The
Adventure Guide
To The
Pacific Northwest

THE ADVENTURE GUIDE TO THE PACIFIC NORTHWEST

Thomas A. Arnold

HUNTER
PUBLISHING, INC.

Printed in Singapore through Palace Press

ISBN 1-55650-034-3

Photographs:

T. A. Arnold: 2, 4, 10, 25, 29, 42, 50, 51, 58, 62,
81, 83, 87, 89, 91, 107, 110, 140, 171, 173, 177, 179,
181, 185, 186, 188, 190. John F. Reginato: 15,
17, 127, 129, 154, 162. Ross Mehan: 46, 71, 96,
98, 99, 103. John Kelly: 113, 117. National Park
Service: 115. Cathy Wilson: 131. Ciro Pena: 147.
Les Bechdel: 149. Washington State Department
of Tourism: 168.

Published in the UK by:
Moorland Publishing Co. Ltd.
Moor Farm Road, Airfield Estate
Ashbourne, Derbyshire DE6 1HD
England

ISBN 086190-243-2

Contents

To Jennifer, Tracey and Jeff, without whose support this book would have been impossible.

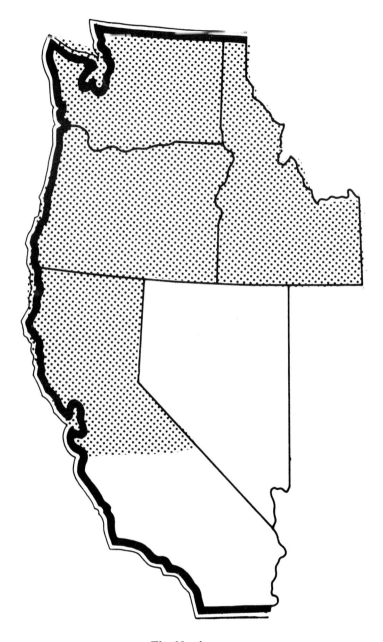

The Northwest

1

WESTERN ADVENTURES

This is a guide for families, business travelers, or anyone seeking outdoor excitement and, above all, fun! Each type of adventure has been given its own chapter and Washington, Idaho, Oregon, and Northern California are covered. This is a vast territory and, to help the reader, a geographical index has been included at the end of the book. At the start of each chapter, there is a regional map showing the location of the adventures to follow.

The trips last from one hour to several days. Some may require camping, while others are perfectly suitable for those with no more than a day to spend. Many business travellers may find this an excellent recreation guide. An adventure trip, even if only for an afternoon, can be the best possible break from a long convention. Most outfitters will supply all equipment necessary for an excursion, and many provide transportation to and from metropolitan areas.

For those who don't have the time to venture away from the cities they may be visiting an urban side-trip may be the answer. Most cities offer bicycle rentals at modest hourly or daily rates. In Chapter 3, Cycling the Blue Line Highways, there is a segment on urban trips. These include 5-, 10-, and 25-mile routes through attractive parks and suburbs in various cities. All of these trips are designed for easy touring. Hill climbs and major thoroughfares are avoided. Other kinds of urban side-trips can be found in Chapters 6, 8, and 9.

Rock climbing requires special skills and equipment.

A LIGHT ADVENTURE

Every adventure trip, no matter what the level of experience required, carries a certain element of risk. That is, of course, what gives it the thrill and excitement. From a white water voyage down Costa Rica's Rio Chirripo to a climb of Yosemite's

North Face, risk is an integral part of the experience. The degree of risk can be controlled by balancing safety factors (the guide, equipment, rules). Some adventures demand special skills, equipment, and experience. Risk factors are high and must be offset by special equipment and training. Imagine sky diving without first knowing how to pack a parachute or land on the ground. Rock climbing, hang gliding, most white water kayaking and canoeing, barrel rides over Niagara Falls, and walks across Death Valley—all these fall in the category of advanced adventures.

Light adventures, on the other hand, begin at a level where little or no experience is needed. These include cycling tours, hot air balloon rides, pack trips through Idaho, and rafting.

Obviously, a gray area exists at the point where the two categories merge. Some adventures, like a gentle trek up Castle Crags or Mt. Lassen, may belong in either category depending on the time of year. In the dead of winter these peaks are packed with snow and can be negotiated only with the aid of special equipment.

Determine your own limits and ability level before leaving, no matter how hard that may seem. It's too late to make this determination when you're half way up the side of a mountain and each step has become an effort in exhaustion.

THE WESTERN REGION—
A DIVERSE GEOGRAPHY

This book covers the Western states of Idaho, Washington, Oregon, and California north from San Luis Obispo. If one word had to be selected to characterize the geography of the region, it would be DIVERSITY. The region contains deserts, massive metropolitan centers, unspoiled beaches, fertile valleys flanked by rolling foothills, and rugged alpine mountains. Each segment of the Western Region offers different opportunities for adventure. When planning an excursion, it helps to have at least a basic understanding of the topography and climate in these sections.

There are five primary geographic areas in the Western Region: 1) the coastal; 2) the coastal mountain; 3) the basins and valleys; 4) the alpine mountains; and, 5) the desert. But what is unique in the West is the way these areas are interwoven and the effect they have on weather conditions.

The geographic boundaries of these areas run north and south, rather than the more typical east/west pattern. Therefore, climatic conditions tend to change as you travel east or west. The average temperature along the northern coast of California and San Diego on the southern coast varies by only two degrees, as one example.

Imagine for a moment you are in a small airplane flying east from the Pacific Ocean. You first encounter a coastal strip that runs from the Canadian border to the Mexican border. In places, such as the Golden Gate in San Francisco, this strip may be very narrow and almost non-existent, while in other portions it may be very broad and feed directly into large basins and valleys. The coastal segment is usually flat and may give rise to gentle rolling hills.

As you fly eastward, you encounter the coastal mountains, commonly referred to as the Coastal Range. In order to pass over this segment, your plane will have to climb to an altitude between 2000 and 8000 feet. As with the coastal segment, this range of mountains extends almost the entire north/south length of the Western Region. They are of non-volcanic origin and support a variety of vegetation—from chaparral and oak woodland in the south to stands of coniferous forest in the north. The Coastal Range terminates at the base of California's Central Valley where the mountains veer eastward to connect with the Sierra Nevada Range. The northern extension runs up past the Canadian frontier.

The next segment includes the great basins and valleys. In California these include the Central, San Joaquin, and Sacramento Valleys; in Oregon, it is the Willamette Valley; and, in Washington, the narrow Puget Sound basin. In most areas, these are rich agricultural communities. Metropolitan centers are located along major transportation and shipping routes, and these are few and far between.

Leaving the valleys, your airplane must climb to great altitudes to cross the mountains that make up the central spine of

---

Whitewater rafting is an adventure for everyone.

the region. In California the Sierra Nevada Range rises to average altitudes greater than 10,000 foot. This range extends 400 miles along the eastern edge of the State. It is an average of 80 miles wide and has the typical characteristics of alpine mountains. At the northern tip of the Sacramento Valley, the Sierra Nevada Range joins with the Cascade Range. These mountains continue this central corridor of high peaks throughout Oregon and Washington. The Cascades are of volcanic origin and include some of the more notable craters: Mt. Saint Helens, Crater Lake, and Mt. Lassen.

The next segment is once again a large basin. But, unlike the fertile valleys prior to the Cascades and Sierra Nevadas, these are large, arid plains, and some are at altitudes of 5,000 feet. In the southern portions east of the Sierra Nevada Range, these basins are actually dry deserts. These include Death Valley, the Mojave Desert, and the Colorado Desert. None of these deserts are included in the scope of this book. They will be left to future volumes covering the Southwest.

Returning to the northern sections of the Western Region, the Columbia Plateau of Washington and the Great Basin of Oregon end near Idaho. At this point, the land rises up into the Bitterroot Mountain Range. This alpine segment hosts more high peaks and is just west of the northern slopes of the Rocky Mountains in central Montana.

As I hinted earlier, the north/south boundaries of these segments have resulted in some highly unusual climatic conditions. Isotherms (zones of relatively the same climate and temperature) generally follow east/west lines of latitude. But in the Western Region, they run almost north and south following the various segments. In winter, inland temperatures tend to be colder when compared to the coast. Many portions of Idaho and the slopes of California's Sierra Nevada range can also experience sub-zero temperatures. In the summer, a high pressure cell moves off the coast and brings off-shore winds. Masses of air funnel through the coastal mountains by way of breeches such as the Golden Gate, Columbia River, and Puget Sound through to the valley segments. In some cases this acts almost as a natural air conditioner, maintaining uniform temperatures along north/south lines.

These isotherms can have a strong effect on the planning of an adventure trip. For example, on a short bicycle tour from San Rafael—a small community nestled in the California wine country—to the rugged Marin Coast, one must be prepared for sometimes drastic temperature shifts. While the eastward city of San Rafael is toasting at a warm 70°, the coast—a mere ten miles west—shivers at 50°. In my younger, more athletic days while running the Bay-to-Breakers race in San Francisco, I experienced the negative effects of this temperature shift. The start of the race along the shores of San Francisco Bay was a mild 68° in the sun. My friends and I were dressed in light jogging clothes. When the starter's gun fired, we ran off eastward through the city streets. I was just running for the fun of it. The only thing on my mind was not stopping, not letting the effects of gravity drive me to a walk. It wasn't until I was entering the eastern gates of Golden Gate park with a mile and a half left in the race that I felt a chill in my arms and legs. My tank top provided little insulation against the off-shore breeze and the approaching fog bank. It was at this moment that I realized why several of the runners back at the starting line had kept their warm up clothes on. Their bodies could deal with the temperature of the first third of the race and would remain comfortably protected against the cold in the last two thirds.

To this day, I still believe that it was this incident that gave me the worst cold that I can remember. Had there not been someone waiting for me at the finish line, I might have been in danger of losing too much body heat—a condition known as hypothermia. A dose of prior planning would have increased the comfort factor and my enjoyment of the event.

TRIP PLANNING

There are a few key elements that should be considered when planning an adventure tour. First, take a close look at the tour "style" you prefer. For instance, the issue whether or not to camp under a bed of stars or beneath a quilt in a bed-and-breakfast inn is a matter of style. Other considerations can be less obvious.

Time How much time is there for the trip? Does the family mind driving for several hours to the river early in the morning on the same day the trip leaves? Or do they require a night's rest before the actual trip? For a self-paced tour, such as cycling, how many miles can you cover in a morning or in a day? Analyzing this is very important and can mean the difference between success and disaster. A key ingredient is not to be over-confident or fool yourself into believing something can be done too easily.

Energy Fatigue can lead you to ignore risks, which can have major side effects. Take the case of a cross-country skier who has exerted too much energy climbing a hill. As the hill slopes downward and the skier picks up speed, a burning sensation begins in the thighs; suddenly, legs feel as though they are filled with cement. This skier is heading for a fall.

Location Consider the distance that must be traveled in order to reach a tour site, as well as the geographic segment within the Western Region. The latter factor is extremely important. Remember my Bay-to-Breakers race in the prior section. That is an example of the effect when crossing isothermal zones. If your trek up Castle Crags begins in a mixed woodland and ends on an alpine summit, consider what the temperature might be on top. When combined, location and type of activity dictate the packing requirements for clothing and miscellaneous gear.

Eating Consider the size, weight, and type of food that your trip will require. If you are taking a short subterranean excursion, food may not be an important factor. But if the trip lasts more than half a day, you should consider what your intake will be prior to, during, and after the activity. One of the best texts on this subject is Chapter Six of Mirkin and Hoffman's, *The Sports Medicine Book.*

Drinking While in the midst of an activity, be it walking, cycling, or paddling, the body loses fluids. This is particularly true in high temperatures. It is estimated that during heavy exercise in hot weather you can sweat and breathe away up to four pounds of water in an hour. This must be replaced constantly, even if you don't feel thirsty. On a bicycle ride, it is wise to drink every few minutes. When the body feels thirsty, it has already lost two to four pounds of fluid.

A key consideration in planning a trip is deciding whether or not to take a guided tour, if the option exists. Several of the trips described in this book can be taken either individually or with a guide. Consider your style of traveling when making this decision. On a guided tour, many of these "style" factors are handled for you. On a raft trip, for example, the tour operator will provide food, water, safety equipment, and vehicle support.

SAFETY AND CONSERVATION

One last word on two very important topics. Safety and a traveler's ability to abide by rules are key factors that make these trips fun. Several of the trips described are led by professional guides and outfitters. If you want to ride in a hot air balloon, they don't just loan one out for a few hours with a set of instructions. The tour operator is left with all the tactical headaches, such as deflating the balloon after a trip and lugging it back for the next group.

The one area that should never be left totally to anyone else is personal safety. During most trips, guides give a brief talk on safety procedures before setting out. By following these rules, the fun factor increases and the risks remain at manageable levels. During any of the self-guided trips described in this book, the entire responsibility for safety is on the shoulders of the participant. While bicycling on a short urban sidetrip, obey all traffic laws. This includes observing those troublesome stop signs, traffic lights, and not running over pedestrians on the sidewalks. It was estimated in one California city that over 80% of the bicycle accidents were actually caused by the bike rider. And, remember, children tend to imitate their parents. So there are educational reasons to remember and follow common-sense safety rules.

Conservation of natural resources such as lakes, rivers, trees, and manmade resources is equally important. Most tour outfitters will remind travelers of these precautions and the laws insuring preservation of these places. However, it is also

Cycling the backroads.

an individual responsibility to be ecologically minded for your-self and others who will be adventuring after you.

As stated before, the goal of this book is to offer fun and exciting alternatives to families seeking outdoor recreation and adventure. Be safe and have fun.

2

CAVE EXPLORING

A CRAWL THROUGH CRYSTAL CAVERNS

It is 9 A.M. The sun is shining brightly over the Sierra foot-hills. Ten persons stand ready to descend into a small hole in the earth. One young girl adjusts the chin strap on her helmet as the leader starts into the cave. To an idle observer it might appear that the group is mining for gold or other precious ore, but that would be wrong. It is simply a guided tour leaving earth's surface to explore the subterranean world. Once beneath the surface and away from natural sunlight, the group activates their bright lanterns and they begin down a well trodden trail. Helmets are worn not so much for protection against the roof falling in as against the likelihood of tall travelers bumping their heads.

As the wash of the lights illuminates the first natural chamber, the group is confronted by the pure white shimmer of a calcite formation. The sparkling crystals stretch across the ceiling and down a wall like sheets of white paper. At one angle, the formation takes on the appearance of the pipes of a cathedral organ. And then, as you depart the chamber, the sculpture seems transformed into an angel, its wings spread in glory.

For a few hours, on either a guided tour or an organized spelunking expedition, you can be taken through lavish cham-

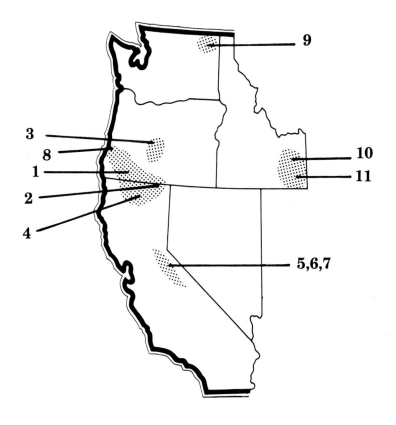

1. Oregon Caves National Monument
2. Lava Beds National Monument
3. Lava River Caves
4. Shasta Caverns
5. Cave City
6. Mercer Caverns
7. Moaning Cavern
8. Sea Lion Caves
9. Gardner Cave
10. Crystal Ice Cave
11. Minnetonka Cave

bers, beholding treasures that have taken millions of years for nature to create. Each formation is unique. Many are named after human or animal forms they resemble, and some display a beauty of stark geometric formations in pure white crystal.

At most caverns, there are three types of tours offered; prices may vary drastically (from free to $55) and the duration of the tours may range from 20 minutes to five hours.

Self guided tours

These are available in a number of State and National Park areas. Trails follow one specific, marked course, and visitors are offered pamphlets that explain the geologic formations. It is up to each traveler to wear warm enough clothing, take along a good lantern, and provide suitable equipment. I might point out that flashlights just don't cut the darkness in a cave. It takes the bright light cast by a lantern (preferably a double-mantle type) or a special miner's light to do the job.

Casual guided tours

A small group is led through the caverns while a guide describes the pertinent history and information surrounding the caves. The tours usually follow manmade trails, and spotlights illuminate the unique mineral formations. No special equipment, aside from comfortable shoes and a warm jacket or sweater, is required.

Spelunking tours

Groups follow natural paths into deeper, more recently discovered chambers. For this, guests are outfitted in coveralls and miner's helmets and follow a guide through the chambers. On a typical trip through Cave City (near Mountain Ranch, California), travelers shimmy through passages on their backs, down rope ladders, and float across underground lakes in a rubber raft.

TOURS AND EXPEDITIONS

Caves are unique in the world of adventure travel. They rarely succumb to external changes in climate and average 50° year round. Therefore, it is wise on any of the trips to wear comfortable shoes and clothing appropriate to the environment. If you suffer from heart or breathing problems or are not able to crouch and do light climbing, a trip beneath the crust may not be for you.

Throughout southern Oregon and most of California, there are numerous caverns and tubes open for public tours. Some of these offer guided walks through well marked trails and illuminated chambers, while others provide the added feature of a spelunking tour for the stout-hearted adventurer.

Here are several locations where travelers and families can venture into underworld caverns:

Oregon Caves National Monument

At the town of Cave Junction (convenient landmark) where Highways 199 and 46 intersect, travel east for approximately 20 miles. The drive alone is well worth the trip as the road winds through tall stands of luscious pine trees. At the 3000 foot level, near the end of the road, the entrance to the cave awaits. Accompanied by a guide, travelers are led through a maze of passageways and through lighted chambers. Unlike many other caverns that are carved out of limestone, the Oregon Caves are in marbled rock. This has resulted in many unique formations such as Neptune's Grotto, Banana Grove, and Paradise Lost. One of the highlights is a miniature stone waterfall. Guided tours depart frequently between 9 A.M. and 5 P.M. every day from May to September. Group sizes are held to 16–20 persons. Children under age 6 are not permitted in the cavern, though child-care may be available.

Lava Beds National Monument

For six months in 1872, a renegade band of 53 Modoc Indians held off 1000 well equipped and trained U.S. Army soldiers. The Indians had been placed on a reservation in southern Oregon along with another tribe of their worst enemies. They left

Schonchin Butte

the reservation to return home to their native lands only to encounter settlers. They dug into positions, and the conflict began. Each time the troops charged the Indians' position, their enemy would vanish through a network of caves, only to reappear at another position in the large meadow to counterattack the soldiers again. The Indians had discovered their own natural Maginot Line in the form of lava tubes.

Upon your first visit to Lava Beds, it is hard to imagine a military conflict being played out amidst such peaceful grazing land. The level country is flanked by only a few cinder cone volcanoes. But once you enter one of the tubes through a massive opening, you come face-to-face with the awesome force and reality of nature. Lava tubes, unlike caves, are formed as a molten lava from an erupting volcano cools. The surface layers solidify into rock, while the lower portions remain liquid. This lower section then continues to flow, leaving a hollow and almost perfectly symmetrical tunnel in its path. There are several ice caves in the park that are also open for public tours. These lava tubes, unlike most caves that maintain a constant temperature of 50°, remain frozen all year. The walls and floors of these caves are covered with a layer of ice.

Lava Beds National Monument is located just south of the Oregon border in Northern California, approximately 35 miles east of U.S. Highway 97. Take the Old State Highway Road turn off to Tennant Road; head north to Tennant Lava Beds Road, which will take you into the monument. It is a long drive from the freeway, and you should plan an entire day for this trip. Naturalists lead daily tours through the tubes at 2 P.M. during the summer season. These guided tours are free of charge. Beyond this, the tubes are open year round for individual exploring. Lanterns can be borrowed from the park rangers when you arrive. Visitors should wear warm clothes and hats (any type from baseball cap to a helmet).

There are 40 improved campsites (vintage 1940) at Lava Beds National Monument. A few motels are within approximately 35 miles in adjacent towns. For more information, contact: Lava Beds National Monument, P.O. Box 867, Tulelake, CA 96134. Telephone: (916) 667-2282.

Lava River Caves

Located approximately 15 miles south of the town of Bend, Oregon off U.S. Highway 97, this lava tube is a little more accessible than those at Lava Beds National Monument. The tube was formed when molten lava ran through the Mount Newberry foothills. It extends for nearly a mile.

The Caves are open from May to September, 9 A.M. to 4 P.M. Lanterns and coveralls are available for a nominal fee. Lodging and food are available in nearby Bend. Guided tour information is available from the Lava Lands Visitors Center. Telephone: (505) 382-5668.

Shasta Caverns

On November 3, 1878, James A. Richardson, an employee of the federal fisheries laid claim to discovering these caverns. Since that time, and until recently, the cavern was explored only by well equipped spelunkers. But once a tunnel was driven through to the first level, this natural museum became open to the public.

Shasta Caves

The caverns are located 20 minutes north of Reading, California off Interstate 5. Take the Shasta Caverns Road turn-off. Guided tours are given daily in the summer (May through Sept. 30) starting at 8 A.M.; and in the winter season at 10 A.M., noon, and 2 P.M. Special group tours and spelunking tours are available. For more information, contact Lake Shasta Caverns, P.O. Box 801, O'Brien, CA 96070. Telephone: (916) 238-2341.

Convenient campgrounds and lodging are available nearby, and there is even a boat dock on Lake Shasta for those coming by water.

Cave City

This is by far the largest and most publicized of the three caverns located in the heart of the California Mother Lode region. These are the same caves that were visited by John Muir, Bret Harte, and Mark Twain. As you walk through these, try to imagine what it might have been like to explore this world with the illumination of only a single candle as they did in the early days. Cave City was also known as the hideout for the notorious bandit Joaquin Murrieta and his gang. Stories persist that his treasure is still hidden in these vast limestone catacombs.

To reach Cave City, take Highway 49 to San Andreas, then head east on Mountain Ranch Road. The caves are open daily from June to October and on weekends during November and December. Guided tours are given between 10 A.M. and 5 P.M. The 5-hour-long Wild Cavern Tour (spelunk tour) leaves at 9 A.M. and is restricted to 10 persons—reservations are a must. For this trip, explorers must be over age 12 and in generally good health; climbing, crawling, and hiking required. For additional information contact: Cave City, P.O. Box 78, Vallecito, CA 95251. Telephone: (209) 736-2708.

No camping is available at Cave City, but there are sites nearby and motels in the vicinity. You should give yourself all day for the spelunking tour and a couple of hours for a guided tour.

Mercer Caverns

These limestone caves boast a wide variety of natural formations in an easily accessible environment. The staff is knowledgeable and the tours are impressive. To reach Mercer Caverns, take Highway 4 to Murphys and follow the signs. Guided tours are offered daily during the summer and on weekends and holidays during the winter. There is a very comfortable picnic area on a hill overlooking the old Shaw Ranch, which is now Stevenot Winery. And after lunch, it's onto a little wine tasting, while the kids have fun climbing on the old mining equipment. Stevenot is well known for its fine gold country Chardonnay.

Campgrounds are nearby, and you can even stay in Ulysses S. Grant's bed at the historic Murphy's Hotel. The hotel restaurant can't be beat. Meals are inexpensive and filling, and they take great care of the young travelers.

For information on cave tours, contact: Mercer Caverns, Box 509, Murphys, CA 95247. Telephone: (209) 728-2101.

Moaning Cavern

This is the last of the three caves in the California gold country. Located off Parrot's Ferry Road between Highway 4 and the city of Sonora, it offers a 45-minute guided tour into the single largest underground chamber in California. Aside from the descent of a 101-foot-long spiral staircase, there is not much physical demand on this tour. But as you stand on the floor of the chamber and look back up at the top, you feel dwarfed by the size. Where you are standing you could easily construct a full-sized 2000-square-foot home. The subterranean scenery is striking and well worth the time to see. This is a perfect side-trip while passing through the Mother Lode. A little further south on Parrot's Ferry Road is the City of Columbia, jewel of the Mother Lode. This town is best remembered for almost becoming the capitol of California. It was the location of the Clint Eastwood film, *Pale Rider.*

For more information about this cavern, contact: Moaning Cavern, P.O. Box 78, Vallecito, CA 95251. Telephone: (209) 736-2708.

Campgrounds are close by, and there are a number of affordable hotels and motels in the Columbia area. One of the better lodgings is the Columbia City Hotel. They only have fifteen rooms and a very fine dining room; you will be staying right off the main street. The hotel is operated by hotel management students of Columbia City College, and they are known to bend over backwards to make your stay extra comfortable. A close friend of mine recently spent his wedding night in the City Hotel and said that it was as enjoyable as staying at a five-star establishment.

Sea Lion Caves

This has been dubbed one of the greatest sea grottoes in the world. The caves have been carved by the sea, which continually flood the cave floor. Visitors are lowered into the cavern by an elevator. From here they are led through the galleries. Pacific sea lions visit the beaches and caves periodically along with numerous species of birds.

Sea Lion Caves is located approximately 12 miles north of the town of Florence on U.S. 101 along the Oregon coast. Lodging is available in nearby Florence and Waldport to the north. These caves are also an easy drive from Eugene, Oregon and would make a nice one-day stop for someone visiting that city.

Tours are offered year round during daylight hours, except on Christmas.

Gardner Cave

This cavern is a portion of the Crawford State Park located 12 miles north of Metaline Falls off State Route 31.Guided tours are offered hourly Monday through Thursday from 10 A.M. to 4 P.M. and Friday through Sunday 10 A.M. to 5 P.M. during the summer months. Visitors to the cave are guided through limestone chambers along an 875-foot passage way.

This state park is located adjacent to the U.S./Canada border in the northeast corner of the State of Washington. The tour is well worth the time for anyone passing through en route to other destinations. Picnic facilities are available at no charge within the park.

Crystal Ice Cave

This lava tube through a volcanic rift is covered with ice formations year round. Much like the caves of Lava Beds National Monument, the grotto was formed as a result of volcanic activity. Due to the configuration of the entrance and the passages below, the temperature remains at a constant 32°.

Guided tours are offered daily between 8 A.M. and 7 P.M. between the months of May and October. This is a commercially operated cave and a modest admission fee is charged.

To reach the Crystal Ice Cave, take Highway 39 north from American Falls, Idaho for approximately 6 miles to North Pleasant Valley Road. Follow Pleasant Valley Road for 22 miles to the entrance of the cave. A portion of this road is unpaved and should be negotiated with care.

Minnetonka Cave

The entrance to this cavern is at an elevation of 7,000 feet above sea level. Inside, however, visitors will discover fossil remains of tropical plants and marine life. How could this be? The guided tour will give you the answer.

Given favorable weather conditions, the cave is open between 9:30 A.M. and 6 P.M., June 13 through Labor Day. Guided tours leave on a regular schedule and cost about $2.50 per person (adults), $1.50 for children ages 6–14.

The Minnetonka Cave is located south of Montpelier. Take Highway 89 south to the town of Saint Charles, then follow the signs for approximately ten miles over an unimproved road to the cave entrance.

Campgrounds and lodging are available in both Montpelier and Saint Charles. There is a small picnic area at the cave.

A FEW WORDS ON SPELUNKING TOURS

Unlike most guided subterranean tours, a spelunking tour is one that travels deeper into less explored areas of a cave and is for the more stalwart traveler.

Most companies offering these trips provide specially trained guides. It is important that you consider some factors when opting to take one of these tours. For instance, find out how much training the guides have had and what is their interest in leading this type of trip. Most of the hard-core spelunkers are involved with the geologic study of caves and their formations. They have had many hours of experience exploring the underground and have a rescue plan in case of trouble. I would be leery of taking one of these trips when there were not at least three other people in the group. My red flag would also go up if there was not a talk given by the guide covering safety procedures prior to the trip. As a general rule of thumb, you should never explore a cave with fewer than four persons, one of whom should be in possession of an advanced first aid and CPR certificate. Well-maintained safety equipment should be provided and include: coveralls, helmets, lanterns, spare power sources, water, and emergency food.

These pointers are only offered as suggestions to help you in selecting a qualified tour guide and outfitter. A good adventure is a safe adventure.

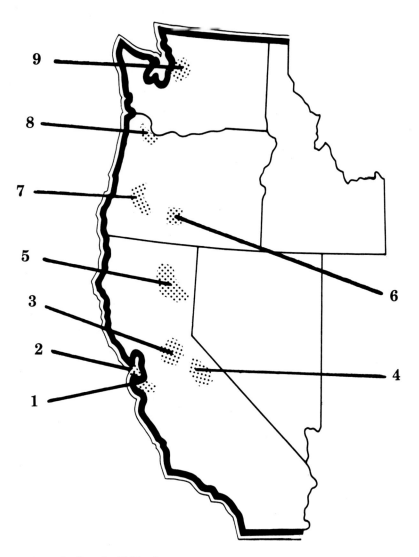

1. Portola Valley Loop
2. Golden Gate Bridge/Sausalito
3. Jedediah Smith National Recreation Trail/Sacramento
4. Cycling the Mother Lode
5. Mt. Lassen and McArthur Burney Falls
6. Rim Drive/Crater Lake
7. Eugene Greenway Bike Trail
8. Sauvie Island/Portland
9. Burke Gilman Bike Trail/Seattle

3

CYCLING THE BLUE LINE HIGHWAYS

There's never been a better feeling than to be rushing down a hillside, the wind blowing at your face and the sun warming your back. You lean gently into each turn and accelerate over a small rise only to race downward once again. Cycling is a silent adventure, much like sailing or soaring in a glider. Aside from the rush of wind, the environment during a ride abounds with the sounds of nature.

Cycling has become one of the Great American pastimes, and one of the best ways to find adventure. While many forms of rapid transport exist to whisk passengers from point A to B, none has so captivated the world as the bicycle.

In 1870, more than fifty years after the invention of the first peddle-wheeled vehicle, James Starley opened the first bicycle company in Britain. His product was the Penny-Farthing, an imposing machine with a 60" diameter front wheel, a petite 20" wheel in the rear, and peddle cranks affixed to the front wheel. This design was intended to increase the power and speed of the vehicle.

The Penny-Farthing was far from the answer to the bicycling needs at the dusk of the nineteenth century. It was a clumsy machine that required a great amount of practice to master. Falls and scraped knees were common place. Eventually, chain drives were added and front-to-rear wheel diameters were equalized.

Since those pioneer days, modern bicycles have become an art of aerodynamic design. Nowadays, the average touring bike can achieve speeds of 20 to 30 miles per hour on a flat stretch, and high-performance racing cycles reach into the low sixties. But the basic pleasure endures of the human-powered machine that moves a man faster than he can walk. This chapter presents the cycling adventure.

Detailed information on trips is split into two sections: self-guided and guided tours. Each of these will offer significant rides in suburban and rural areas. The first two sections are classified according to whether the terrain is typically flat, moderate, or steep. This subjective rating is based on an average over the entire course and is intended to assist in making a final trip selection.

This book lists rides that are optimal for the light adventure. The selection criteria included rideability, terrain, geographic location, accessibility, and exceptional scenery. The appendix in the back of the book offers a reference list where individuals can obtain additional information from local tourism boards and other organizations in a specific region.

PREPARING FOR THE CYCLING ADVENTURE

Tour Style

Each individual traveler has a particular style that is directly related to personal comfort. This isn't a matter of wearing the most fashionable skins while in the saddle, but rather of the overall nature of the trip. For instance, several tours can be taken where the cyclist carries very little gear. Overnight stays may be in motels or stylish bed-and-breakfast inns. Or you may opt to carry tents, sleeping bags, and complete camping gear on the bike and rough it by the side of the road or in a small camp ground. A third option would be to let a tour guide transport luggage and gear, while you worry about only the ride and scenery.

There are some basic questions that should be asked when analyzing style: 1) Do you plan to ride for more than one day?

Cyclists emerge from a wine-country hotel at the start of another day.

2) Will you camp or stay in motels? 3) If camping, how will gear be transported? 4) How will meals be provided? Also, 5) how far do you plan to ride each day? The answer to this last question will help you determine a pace.

Each style has its own merits and unique set of problems. As an example, while cycling through the lush vineyards of the Alaxander Valley in California, I encountered another cyclist on the road near Geyserville. It was a remarkably clear morning, not a cloud in the sky, and the air was crisp and clear. As I pulled up beside him, I observed that his clothing was splattered with dried mud, and his bike along with the side panners (nylon packs that fit on a frame on either side of the front and rear tires) were also coated with the same dirt. We struck up a conversation, talking casually about the countryside and where each of us was heading. Finally, I gave in to my curiosity and asked how he came to look so dirty on such a lovely day. Had he fallen into the Russian River? He returned a broad grin, and said that it had been a remarkably tough night hiding from a sudden rain squall under a wooden picnic table. After all, who would have guessed that there would be a late season rain squall. His tour style involved camping out under the stars. He packed lightly in every respect, including contingency funds.

For some travelers, the inconvenience of a midnight rain shower is all part of the trip. But the lack of preparedness can also spell trouble. My fellow cyclist could have been in far worse condition had he not found his picnic table shelter.

Route Planning

After deciding on a tour style, the next step is to select a suitable route. Much as in planning a motor trip, you will have to consider first where you are coming from and going to, and what is the best route. Usually bike trips are motivated by more than just a desire to go cycling. Motives include visiting a town or museum, or maybe taking in a local festival. Whatever the reason, there is most likely a time schedule to be met.

After considering where point A and B are, it is time to select the actual route. One of the foremost considerations is the topography. As was discussed in the introduction, the West is made up of valleys and basins separated by rolling foothills and high mountain passes. The characteristics of a course will be determined by these geographical elements as well as the type of road and ambient weather conditions. This will also determine the type of equipment and clothing you take along.

There are two ways to approach route planning. You can select a route from a book such as this one and simply study the courses that are outlined. Or you can plan the route from scratch. Most of us, when thinking of route maps, choose a simple highway map from any gas station or automobile club. There is one major problem in this, though: the maps rarely tell you where the hills start and finish. This can be a critical factor in planning a day's ride, especially if the trip encompasses more than one day, and you are trying to reach a lodging site. There is nothing more frustrating, when a plan calls for a 100-mile-per-day pace, than to encounter the unexpected hill climb near the end. Not only is this frustrating but very demoralizing. Your cycling trip may now leave the realm of a light adventure as you struggle up the interminable hillside with darkness falling fast.

Planning the custom trip takes some basic research. You will want to consider topography and relative traffic volumes on the roads that look best. Neither of these are usually found on the basic highway map. Start by finding a well-stocked sporting goods store that caters to backpackers and cyclists. Here you will be able to obtain topographic maps for most of the Western United States. These maps illustrate roads over gradient lines. Depending on the map, the lines might represent 50- or 100-foot vertical changes in altitude. When the gradient lines are shown closer together, the hill is steeper. In reading these maps, identify where hill climbs begin and end.

Another excellent source for route planning material is the local County or State Highway Department. More than likely, if you approach them with a smile, you will get any information you need about a road within their jurisdiction. They can tell you which roads don't allow bicycles, the areas of high traffic flow, and busy truck routes that you'll want to avoid. County offices are spread throughout each state and are, of course, responsible for a smaller network of roads. They are unlikely to know about a road outside of their area.

After considering topography and selecting roads that are suitable to your individual riding abilities, it is important to consider where a day's ride will actually begin and end. Ask yourself how you will reach the starting point. Will you be setting out directly from the bicycle rental agency or driving to the starting point? In the latter case, suitable parking arrangements have to be considered. A year ago, while participating in an organized ride across the Golden Gate Bridge with a return on the San Francisco Bay ferry, one rider left his car on private property. He thought that since it was a Sunday nobody would care. The tow charge was $64 dollars plus cab fare to get him to the storage yard. Not a happy ending.

Next, consider the end of the ride. In the case of most one-day excursions this may be the same as the starting point. But, in an overnight trip, you will be considering suitable camping or lodging. If you are staying at motels or other hostels, your end points will be linked to a very specific geographical location—many times a city. If you are roughing it and camping out, you might be tempted just to ride until you find a place to pitch your tent. Don't do it. There's nothing worse than riding through a gentle valley after a series of hill climbs with the sun setting only to find nothing but barbed wire fences and no trespassing signs. Private property is just that, and most land owners look disdainfully upon people who don't respect their privacy.

In planning the overnight stay, the end of the day's ride should center upon some discernible site. There are numerous State and National Parks, Forest Service lands, private campgrounds, and other local public facilities to choose from. Don't shy away from contacting a private land owner and requesting permission to spend the night. Any request of this nature should be accompanied by a commitment to clean up and leave the land as you found it.

Equipment

For the purposes of this book, we will concern ourselves with two categories of equipment, bicycle and clothing. Other items such as sleeping bags, tents, cooking and kitchen equipment can be included as the need arises. If you do consider camping out while on a ride, select clothing that is light weight and suitable for the anticipated weather conditions. It might help to prepare as though for a backpacking trip, keeping in mind that the weight is not on your shoulders but on your legs as you peddle down the road.

Bicycles

There are a wide variety of touring and racing bikes available. I would not even attempt in a book of this nature to analyze the various makes, models and types. The concern regarding the bicycle is the gearing and type of equipment carried on the bike. For touring the Northwestern Region, you will want to consider obtaining a light touring bike that is equipped with at least ten speeds. This will give you a wide enough selection of gears to meet most conditions you may encounter. By selecting a combination of front and rear gears while riding, you can make peddling up the side of a hill easier or, on flat stretches, increase your speed.

There are a few items that should be carried on the bike. Wear a helmet; carry a first aid kit; take at least one spare

A tour guide checks the equipment before a ride.

inner-tube or sew-up tire, depending on the type; also a one-liter water bottle; enough tools to complete a tire change; personal identification and a few dollars in cash and quarters for an emergency purchase or phone call; a small rag; and, an air pump. If you are riding with a group of people, each person should carry a spare tire and water, but only one of the group need be burdened with the first aid kit and tools.

Clothing

The type of clothing you select can make the difference between an enjoyable ride and a disastrous experience. Two factors affect decisions about clothing in the planning stage: (1) What are the predicted weather conditions? (2) How long will the tour last?

Many people think the answer to the first question is quite obvious. If the weather will be warm, dress light, and vice versa for the cold. The problem is that many people do not consider what is happening when their bodies perspire during vigorous exercise. While preparing for a simple training ride in the early morning, I dressed quickly in a black polo-shirt and cycling britches. The ride took me through rolling foot-hills over a distance of fourteen miles. I was fine through the first two-thirds. But, near the end, the sun was very high, I was sweating, consuming most of my one-liter of water, and feeling hot and run down. I stopped under the shade of a tree and quickly realized that I had dressed wrong for the weather. The dark shirt absorbed the sun's radiation and, just as bad, the polo-shirt I had selected was cotton/polyester mix and did not allow adequate ventilation. To finish the ride, I soaked down the back of my shirt and neck with water. Had I been on a long trip through one of the desert areas of Southern Califor-nia, I might have suffered from heat exhaustion or worse.

Planning for a cold weather ride is just as important. Throughout the summer season, thousands of cyclists enjoy riding across the Golden Gate Bridge from San Francisco to Sausalito (this ride is described later in this chapter). The problem with this seven mile jaunt is that the typical summer weather can include unpredictable fog that socks in the bridge and leaves everything else sunny. Often, it comes up with little or no warning and may bring with it chilly westerly winds.

For cold conditions, the concept of layering works very well. You must consider where your body will lose most of its warmth and then protect that part. The scalp, back of the neck, and groin areas are the most important. The body of a cyclist generates heat and perspiration even when the weather is near freezing. This may lead to wet garments and a loss of important body warmth.

In moderately cold conditions, similar to those encountered on the Golden Gate Bridge, I consider wearing a cotton sweat shirt over my regular cycling shirt, with a light wind breaker over the top. The cycling shirt absorbs most of my sweat, and whatever gets through to the second layer is also absorbed. Being 100% cotton, the sweat shirt still provides insulation when it is damp and also allows some ventilation. The outer windbreaker stops most external moisture from giving you a double drenching.

In conditions where very low temperatures are encountered, the sweatshirt can be replaced by a wool sweater. You might also wear a knit ski cap under your helmet to protect your scalp and a light scarf around your neck that can be pulled up over your mouth and nose. Legs should be protected by long cycling pants. Some people wear leg warmers outside the pants. And recently, exercise tights as a second layer closest to the skin have become quite common.

Whatever you plan for clothing you must consider the length of the ride. This raises the question of how you store the clothing you're not wearing. Through sections of Washington and Oregon, sudden rain storms are common in the summer months. These squalls can last from one to several hours. There's nothing worse than having to make an unscheduled stop to hide under a tree because you didn't bring rain gear. Pack light but take the essentials.

Most important, invest in a comfortable pair of riding britches. These come in a variety of sizes and styles. There are sleek racing pants with every color stripe imaginable running down the legs or there are lighter touring shorts. Whichever you select, they should have a chamois in the groin area as an additional pad against the saddle. As in horseback riding, saddle abrasions can be your biggest problem. Even though I wear the long cycling britches, I still use a coating of Vaseline on my groin and legs during long trips. The pants protect against most abrasions, but skin-to-skin friction may still occur.

Lastly, consider the type of shoes you wear. They should fit easily into your toe clips and be constructed with a firm sole to give support. Beyond this, the type and style are up to your pocket book.

Contingency plans

While on the road, be mentally prepared with a plan for the problems that could arise. In this section, I have listed a few of the more important areas that require consideration.

Weather

Riding in the Northwest can be an exciting experience because of the diversity of landscapes and environment. But the changeable weather that goes with that diversity poses two primary threats to cyclists: hypothermia, a loss of internal body temperature due to cold conditions; and heat exhaustion brought on by high external temperatures and loss of body fluids.

During a short suburban ride, these factors can easily be planned for and carrying extra equipment is usually not necessary. It is important, though, to know when to take action. When your body recognizes the symptoms of either heat exhaustion or hypothermia, it may be too late to correct the problem without help from a fellow cyclist.

For longer rides which cross from one climate segment to another, riders must plan for surprise encounters with changing weather conditions. This may mean carrying a small pack with a sweater or rain gear.

Breakdown

The primary breakdown to plan for is an encounter with an errant piece of glass. The resulting blow-out is usually minor, although some can tear into a new tire. You should carry a small, lightweight tool pouch with a few tire irons and at least one spare inner-tube. It is a lot easier to change an inner-tube at the side of the road than to patch it.

Other problems may include broken spokes, snapped brake cables, or frame damage after a fall. On longer rides through rural areas, it is important to carry a few additional tools for roadside repairs. There is an excellent pocket-size manual covering this topic by Tom Cuthbertson and Rick Morrall—*The Bike Bag Book.*

Beyond making temporary repairs, it is important to know where to get assistance. Bike shops often give aid to cyclists in need of a helping hand, and a gas station may have tools so that you can straighten a frame or a bent peddle.

First Aid

Everyone should know how to administer Cardio Pulmonary Resuscitation (CPR); how to recognize and treat hypothermia and heat stroke; and what to do if a fall results in a broken bone. The American Red Cross or the American Heart Association chapters located throughout the United States offer free or low cost courses in these topics.

On a recent organized 50-mile ride through the foothills of

the San Francisco Bay Area, the mercury rose sharply to the 90s by mid-morning. After passing through the cool shade of an overpass, one of the riders in our group started weaving like a drunk driver and complained of a headache and nausea. We stopped and rushed him into the shade of a small shrub by the roadside, then soaked his head and neck with water from our bottles. After a few minutes, he was feeling much better. We gently rode to a store a mile away and bought drinks to replenish his water loss.

Filing a "Trip Plan"

Much in the same manner that an airplane pilot lets the air traffic controllers know what his departure time, course, speed and arrival time is, you can let a friend know what course you're riding and what time you're due back. Many times a delay may be the result of a mechanical failure. It's a nice feeling to know that if you're stranded someone will be along to look for you.

Transporting a bicycle

Taking something the size of a bicycle on a common carrier is a lot easier than it may seem. There are only two real concerns: 1) shipping the bike so as to minimize possible damage; and, 2) doing it at the lowest cost.

Cost depends on the type of transportation you select. Many local transit agencies have special regulations regarding the carrying of bicycles. It would be advisable to call the local agency and check. Of course, this is for local travel only. What about the major, long distance carriers?

Airlines

Most of the national air carriers allow ticketed passengers to check a bicycle as part of their luggage. There is a small fee ($25) to cover extra handling and most will supply a cardboard container. No parts of the bicycle may protrude from the box. This means that you will have to remove or turn the handle bars so they are parallel with the frame; remove the front wheel; and take off the peddles. Also, let the air out of both tires, since most of the baggage compartments are not pressurized, and wrap the rear derailer with a few heavy rags to protect it from clumsy baggage handlers.

Rail

For a $5 fee, Amtrak provides a bicycle box and will check a bike into the baggage car. The same precautions apply as described above. If your train trip takes you to a small depot without a full-time staff, make certain that you see the bike off-loaded by the train crew. I was debarking once in Truckee, California when, just as the train was leaving, I realized that my skis were still on it. The station master wired the next station and I had to wait a day for my skis to be returned.

Bus

Various bus companies have different procedures for handling bicycles. Greyhound allows all ticketed passengers to check two pieces of luggage and carry on one. If the bicycle is boxed, they will allow travelers at no extra charge to check it as one of their allowable pieces of luggage.

On the highway

Riding Smart

There are a few factors that will almost guarantee a safe adventure. In a nutshell, they are to ride smart by obeying all traffic laws and always wear a helmet. I have seen many riders disregard these every day, and occasionally one ends up in the local emergency room. Along with wearing helmets, many highway laws appear to be a great inconvenience to cyclists. The stop sign on the quiet residential street or the traffic light that won't trigger when a bicycle crosses its sensor are the most common frustrations. Some bike riders decide to act like a motorist some of the time and a pedestrian the rest. Most drivers can anticipate the movements of other vehicles according to accepted rules of the road. It is when the unexpected violation occurs that accidents result. One sobering statistic to remember about highway safety is that over 80% of the auto/bicycle accidents are the fault of the cyclist.

SELF-GUIDED CYCLING TOURS

Portola Valley Loop (25 or 50 miles)

This is one of the most popular cycling routes in the San Francisco Bay Area and possibly within the entire State of California. Several cycling clubs and the American Heart Association use the course for annual tours.

The route can begin at several locations. I prefer to start at Foothill College where parking is readily available (be sure to pay the 50¢ fee to avoid a citation). To reach the college from I-280 at Los Altos, take the El Monte/Moody Road off-ramp and head approximately 1/4 mile west. El Monte Road drives directly onto the campus. Park your vehicle in the lot directly on your left as you enter the campus.

On your bicycle, you will exit the college at the west gate intersection of Moody Road and Elena. Turn right on Elena. You immediately begin climbing gradual hills as you absorb the warm surroundings of Los Altos Hills. The road winds through the lovely ranch style homes, then curves downward, coming to an end at Purissima. Turn left and ride the short distance to Arastradero where you will again turn left. Crossing under the I-280 freeway, you will start up a short but steep hill until you reach Page Mill Road. This is a major intersection and you should turn left. Be careful of traffic coming off the freeway ramps. This is one of the busiest intersections you will cross. You will ride for a very short distance on Page Mill. Make the first right turn onto the northern leg of Arastradero Road. This road is much quieter and is punctuated by several short climbs and down hill sections. It is usually shady under the tall rows of eucalyptus trees that line the shoulders, and there are many nice resting spots along the way.

Arastradero ends at Alpine Road. The "Alpine House" a particularly famous bar and grill is on the south west corner of this intersection. It's a good place to meet friends before or after the ride. At this point, you will turn left and follow Alpine Road through the town of Portola Valley. After riding about a mile, you will reach Portola Road, where you should turn right. After a quarter mile, you start down a long down hill. The surface of the bike lane varies a bit so try to control

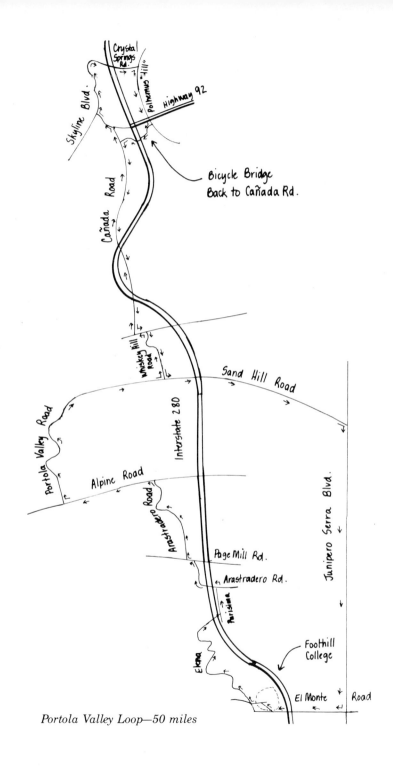

Portola Valley Loop—50 miles

your speed. Ahead, Portola Road turns into Sand Hill Road; no action is needed—just keep enjoying the down-hill ride.

As you leave the mixed woodlands of the foothills and enter the grasslands surrounding the Stanford Linear Accelerator, begin watching for the intersection of Whiskey Hill Road. This marks the splitting point between the 25-mile and 50-mile rides. If you want the shorter of the two rides, disregard the next few paragraphs and pick up the narration as we return to Sand Hill Road.

Your left turn onto Whiskey Hill Road leads you into the rustic town of Woodside. As the road ends in front of the Wells Fargo Bank, turn left and continue the short distance to Canada Road, where you will turn right. For the return trip to Sand Hill, you will be reversing this sequence. Canada Road leads you through the heartland of the San Francisco Peninsula. You pass by several beautiful ranch estates (including Filoli where Dynasty is filmed) and travel over hills adjacent to the Crystal Springs reservoir. The scenery and scent of wild flowers has made this route extremely popular. In fact, the road is closed to motor vehicles on the first and third Sundays during the summer just so cyclists can enjoy it.

The road ends at Highway 92. You will turn left here and coast down a short hill. Take the first right turn. The road is poorly labeled, but this will be Skyline Blvd. Follow this a short distance until you are under a large bridge where the I-280 freeway crosses above. For that matter, you will probably be studying the bridge and not even notice that you just cycled over the San Andreas Dam. Turn right onto Crystal Springs Road. The course continues downhill at this point and, as they say, whatever goes down must come up.

Crystal Springs Road ends, and you will take a sharp right turn onto Polhemus Road. Be prepared: this is a steep, sustained hill climb for nearly a mile. You may want to stop for water at the gas stations along this road and refill your water bottle. Not only is this the halfway point of the ride but it is also the last water stop until you return to the town of Woodside.

After crossing over Highway 92, you will see a small parking area off to the right and a paved path along this hillside. This is the Canada bike trail. It makes a nice downhill run, and you will surely feel like letting go and gliding, but hold back. This path has a few hazards that you will need to steer around. It will lead you to a special bicycle over-crossing of Interstate 280 and back to Canada Road. At this point you will reverse the course until you ride through Woodside and reach Sand Hill Road.

If you are taking the 25-mile course, turn right at Sand Hill Road and begin the last of your "give a grunt" hills. After Polhemus, this one will seem simple. In a short distance, the road starts downward and, after crossing back over Interstate 280, widens into four lanes, You will be traveling about a mile and a half. Santa Cruz Avenue is the major intersection at the bottom where the four-lane portion of the road ends. Be extra careful through here. This is a major intersection with very narrow shoulders to ride on. Needless to say, you will have to mix in with the cars at this point. Turn right onto Santa Cruz and get into the left lane. At the next light, which is just around the bend (about 100 yards), you will be turning left. Only the left lane is allowed to turn, so be sure not to miss it. You will be turning onto Junipero Serra Blvd., which will become Foothill Expressway after a few miles. There are nice wide bike lanes through the rest of the trip so take it easy; cool your heels and enjoy the sights of Stanford University.

You will ride on Junipero Serra/Foothill Expressway for approximately 6 miles until you reach El Monte. Turn right here to complete the Portola Valley loop with a gentle, 2-mile climb back to Foothill College.

Golden Gate Bridge/Sausalito (15 miles one way; ferry return)

This is the perfect ride for business travelers or families visiting the "city by the bay". San Francisco has many resources including great restaurants, cable cars, attractive shopping areas, and bicycle rentals. The Golden Gate Bridge is also one of the few spans that provides separate lanes for cars, pedestrians, and bicycles. Well, at least this is the case on weekends. On weekdays, bicycles may also use the pedestrian path. But for this trip, you are better suited staying on the bike side, or west side of the bridge.

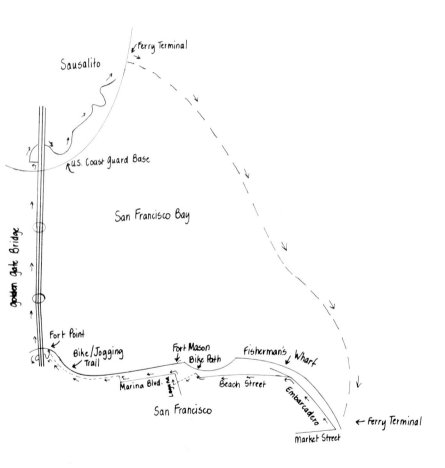

Golden Gate Bridge/Sausalito—15 miles one way

To start the ride, park your vehicle close to the Ferry Building (or, World Trade Center as its sign now reads), at Market and Embarcadero Streets. This is also where the ride will end with your return passage on the Golden Gate Ferry. This route begins along Fisherman's Wharf, a setting for many motion pictures and a San Francisco favorite. If you take this ride on a weekend, park your car a block or so away on one of the side streets intersecting Market Street. Parking restrictions here are not enforced on Saturday or Sunday, as they are at the waterfront. Should you travel this route on a weekday, be prepared to pay over $7 for a parking space. Also, San Francisco tends to be rather ruthless on their enforcement of parking violations. You could very well find at the end of a pleasant ride that your vehicle has been towed.

I would suggest starting this ride before 10:00 A.M. Fisherman's Wharf and Fort Point areas get busy with tourist traffic, and you can't really enjoy the scenery if you're dodging cars whose drivers are preoccupied by the same scenery.

Begin by riding north along the Embarcadero, past the shipping ports and into the heart of the Wharf. Continue until the Embarcadero ends at Taylor Street. At this point, you will turn left for a block, and then right onto Jefferson. This road will end for motor vehicles, but continues as a wide, paved path to the waterside of the maritime museum. Follow this path to its end. At this point, just before it starts out onto the municipal piers, another path (actually a closed road) takes off to the left (west). This path makes a short but steep climb through Fort Mason. At the top, the pavement ends and gives way to a rideable gravel path. Follow this to the exit along Marina Blvd. This attractive and heavily traveled road fronts the Marina Green and the Saint Francis Yacht Club. There is a nice bike path adjacent to the road on the bay side. It provides a break from having to deal with the traffic, but watch out for pedestrians. This path is a favorite of joggers in the city. Near the end of the Green, before the gates of Crissy Field, the path appears to end. Stay to the right at this point and turn on either Lyon Street or Marine Drive. You will pick up the path again later. Unfortunately, the path at this point is gravel, and will remain so until you reach Fort Point. Ride with care.

Should you miss the turn at the end of the Green, worry not. There are several suitable routes to the Bridge from this point. Just ride on through the open gates. Crissy Field is a part of the San Francisco Presidio, an active U.S. Army base that is open to the public. At this point, you are now riding on Mason Street. If you are not in the mood for a hill climb, follow Mason to Hamilton Street where you will have to turn right. Here you can once again access the path to Fort Point.

Those looking for a hill climb, can turn onto Crissy Field Drive (left off of Mason, just after Livingston Street). The climb will begin almost immediately as you ride up to Lincoln Blvd. Turn right onto Lincoln and continue climbing. You will pass by attractive homes which make up part of the officers' quarters. Take the right turn just prior to crossing under the U.S.-101 freeway. This will be the scenic vista stop (a large parking area) above Fort Point, at the Golden Gate Bridge toll plaza.

For those who have stayed the course and remained on the Marina path, you will approach the main gates of Fort Point. This National Historic Park is located directly beneath the Golden Gate Bridge. It is a classic brick fortress that was built in the early nineteenth century to guard the entrance to San Francisco Bay. Portions of it have been restored and are open for public viewing. As you approach the fort, watch for a series of stone steps along the left that go up toward the bridge. You will have to stop and walk your bike up this path. At the top, you will step onto the scenic overlook at the bridge's toll plaza. Once you reach the bridge, follow the signs to the bicycle path on the west side. The ride across the bridge affords views of San Francisco, the islands in the bay, Mount Tamalpais to the north, and the turbulent waters of the Pacific Ocean. Be prepared for sometimes heavy, offshore cross winds or fog. Most of the ride is in relatively moderate temperatures, except for the bridge crossing. Due to the wind and cold fogs, this can be a chilling experience. Conditions usually warm up once you reach the Marin Headlands.

As you approach the Marin anchorage of the bridge, watch for a cement pedestrian ramp that runs off to the left at a right angle to the bridge. Take this ramp to a small, paved path that you will follow in a northerly direction. Crossing through a fence, the path opens onto a road that circles back under the bridge. From this point it is a nice downhill ride into down-town Sausalito. As you ride through another open military base (U.S. Coast Guard), just ride straight ahead and stay on the same road. There are signs directing you toward Sausalito.

The route ends at the ferry terminal in the heart of this modest town. There are several fine restaurants along the main street, and you will find a suitable bicycle rack in front of the ferry terminal. The Golden Gate Ferry runs several times each day. As the schedules occasionally change, it would be worthwhile to check at the ticket booth for times. On my last trip, the return passage was less than $5.

Jedediah Smith National Recreation Trail/ Sacramento (suburban tour; 23 miles one way)

This trip takes you off the traveled roads and onto a trail de-signed in 1896 for bicycle traffic. The route meanders along the banks of the American River, through the heart of the State Capitol, and ends at the shore of Folsom Lake.

The trail begins in Old Sacramento along the banks of the Sacramento River. Old Sacramento exists today as the phoenix of ghost towns. Once a thriving city during the gold rush, it

Cycling is a self-paced sport. You can enjoy the back country at your own speed.

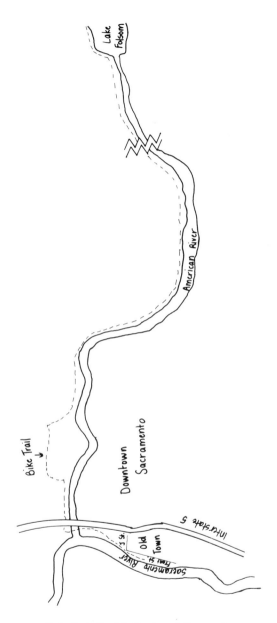

Jedediah Smith National Recreation Trail/Sacramento—23 miles one way.

of ghost towns. Once a thriving city during the gold rush, it was later reduced to a slum district during the depression era. Through careful planning and skillful renovation, the old buildings sparkle again, and the history of this golden city has returned to life.

A pay parking lot within walking distance of the trail head is located along Front Street on the Sacramento River side of the town. During weekends, this can be quite crowded with visitors. From this point, the trail leads north on the top of a levee. After about a mile, the trail turns eastward as you approach the mouth of the American River. You will merge with traffic at Jiboom Street and make a left turn onto a steel girder bridge. Once on the other side of the bridge, you enter Discovery Park, once the home of the Nisenan Maidu Indians, a tribe that hunted and fished in the area before the appearance of the Europeans. The trail makes a sharp right turn and is marked by a small wooden sign. It crosses beneath the new I-5 freeway overpass, and then straightens out along the northern levee.

Several gentle hills lie ahead, and numerous scenic points await your arrival. Though most of the original sites have vanished, you will ride through the same tracts where Jedediah Smith first camped and set out his traps. It was his accounts of the quality of furs that led many trappers to follow in his footsteps. Further up river, you cross the site where John Sutter built his first ranch. He later obtained the land grant to build Sutter's fort at this spot. A few more miles pass, and you enter upon the site where John Sutter assigned James Marshall to build a lumber mill near the town of Coloma. The wheels of destiny were in motion; the next event was the discovery of gold. At the end of the 23 miles, you reach the wooded shores of Folsom Lake. It's time for a rest and maybe a light lunch before the return trip.

Cycling the Mother Lode (various rural tours; distances range from 2 to 36 miles)

The State of California Department of Parks and Recreation publishes a small pamphlet entitled, "Bicycling Through the

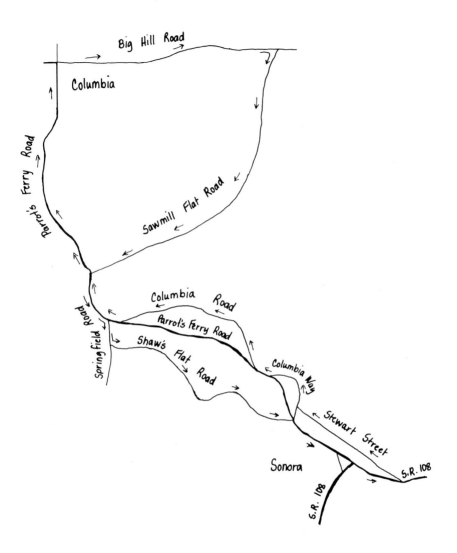

Mother Lode Columbia to Sonora—6 or 8.5 miles roundtrip

Mother Lode". It contains detailed maps and information on 22 tours.

This region of California attracts visitors from throughout the world who come to see the relics of the Old West. Several historic towns where miners staked their livelihood on gold flakes and an occasional nugget have been restored. The spirits of these pioneers live on in the hearts of every visitor who saunters up to the oak bar in the Saint James Saloon in Columbia, or who stays the night in Ulysses S. Grant's room in Murphy's Diggings.

Though the gold veins have died out and little remains of the miners except monuments, the lure today is the open countryside of these foothill communities. In the shadow of the Sierra Nevada Mountains, the California Mother Lode provides the ideal region for cycling. There's something for everyone: from challenging courses with steep hill climbs to gentle trails that wind around the hills.

A favorite route leads cyclists around a gentle 6-mile loop through the town of Columbia. The entire city has been dedi-

Artifacts from the Gold Rush, such as this stamp mill, are visible from the backroads throughout the Mother Lode.

cated as a State Historic Park. No motor vehicles are allowed on the main street, and many residents dress in the attire of the mid-1800's on weekends. Near the center of the town is a working blacksmith's shop where tools and horse shoes are molded from raw materials.

The Columbia bike ride begins at the intersection of Italian Bar Road and Big Hill Road. This is the beginning of the main street of the town. On the northeast corner, stands the Saint James Saloon, and across the street is a parking area where you can leave your car. Start this loop ride by following Big Hill Road east out of town. This is a gradual hill and not too difficult. After 1 1/2 miles, the road levels and intersects Sawmill Flat Road on the right. Turn here and follow it around through the new portions of the town and back to Parrot's Ferry Road. To complete the loop, turn right and return the mile and a half back to Big Hill Road. If you feel energetic, you can turn left and Parrot's Ferry Road will lead you to the city of Sonora. Parrot's Ferry Road is the main arterial road leading into Columbia and can be heavily traveled during peak hours. Cyclists should watch for truck and auto traffic.

The Columbia to Sonora loop is also described in the pamphlet and adds 8 1/2 miles to the ride. If you ride this route in the summer and early fall, carry water and prepare for warm, dry temperatures. This applies to most of the rides in the Mother Lode. You may want to consider these trips in the early morning or late afternoon, before the shade is hidden by the bright Sierra sun.

Mt. Lassen and McArthur Burney Falls (rural trip with hills; 52 miles one way)

This is one of the most enjoyable rides in Northern California. The scenery is mixed between the volcanic mountain tops and the dense, green forests along the way. It begins at the interpretive center in Lassen National Park, just inside the main gate off of State Highway 89.

The elevation of the entire ride varies between 4000 and 5000 feet. For some people just arriving from the valleys, this may create a bit of a problem and require a few days to acclimate. Highway 89 has only a gravel shoulder in the area usu-

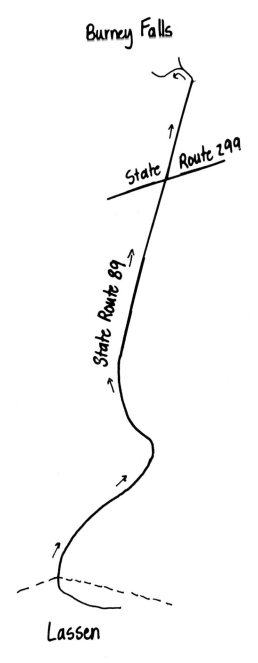

Burney Falls

State Route 299

State Route 89

Lassen

Mt. Lassen/Burney Falls State Park—52 miles one way

ally paved for cyclists, and it can be heavily traveled by tourists on weekends and loggers on weekdays.

A suggestion on dealing with logging trucks: you will hear them before they reach you. The trucks are usually loaded with timber, driven at or above the speed limit, and spraying bark and wood chips in their wake. When you hear them, you would be well advised to pull off and stop on the shoulder until they pass.

The first leg of the tour climbs to a pass and, at the summit (5905 feet above sea level) starts down through the Lassen National Forest. This is a particularly attractive stretch. The somewhat stark, volcanic landscape of Lassen Park gives way to dense pine forests. The air is heavy with the sweet scent of Sugar Pine trees, and an occasional breeze rustles the branches of the trees in an orderly array. From the saddle of a bicycle, Highway 89 takes on a new dimension. Suddenly, life abounds in the forest when there is little or no auto traffic to disturb it. I have observed badgers, countless squirrels and chipmunks, small lizards, jays and a host of other birds while on this stretch of road.

The small town of Hat Creek provides a welcome rest stop along the way. The general store is well stocked, and you will be able to refill your water bottle before proceeding.

Leaving Hat Creek, the highway begins a gradual climb until reaching the main entrance of McArthur Burney Falls State Park. This is a great place to camp and an equally fantastic place to visit. The foremost attraction is the falls. 200,000,000 gallons of water pour down a 100-foot cliff every 24 hours. As you gaze upon the waterfall from the vista, it is hard to imagine that the source is an underground river that surfaces only a quarter mile upstream. There is a nice 1-mile hike to the base of the falls; this is an excellent place to take refuge from the summer heat after a long ride.

This state park is also equipped with a grocery store and snack shop where you can buy supplies for the evening or just enjoy a cool soda. At this point, you can ride back over the same route back to Mt. Lassen, or proceed north on Highway 89 into the town of Mt. Shasta and the connection with Interstate 5. The latter adds another 50 miles and contains several nice hill climbs. Usually after reaching Burney Falls, I have a

MacArthur Burney Falls—
a welcome sight
after the ride from Mount
Lassen.

friend drive my van there and we either push-on or spend the
night.

Rim Drive/Crater Lake (33 mile loop road, heavily traveled on weekends)

This can only be described as a majestic ride. The water surrounding Wizard Island is the richest royal blue, and the tiny
ripples along its surface sparkle like a thousand diamonds on
a sunny afternoon.

The ride begins from the Visitor's Center. Here cyclists can
take a moment to enjoy presentations on the geologic history
of the park and prepare for the tour. It is advisable to fill water
bottles at this point as there is limited water available along
the course.

Rim Drive is a one way road in a clockwise direction around
the lake. To start, turn right as you exit the Visitor's Center
parking lot. The road makes several gentle climbs as it winds
around the few peaks that remain of the once 12,000 foot tall
Mount Mazama that exploded to form the lake. Now, none of
them rise over 8200 feet.

One of the magnificent views of Crater Lake from Rim Drive.

This route is at a high altitude, so cyclists who are not adapted to the elevation should take their time. Fortunately, this is well-heeded advice because of the stunning views offered as you ride. Another adverse factor can be the changeable weather. Rim Drive is only open during the summer, and most travelers would expect the weather to be warm. This may not always be the case as thunder storms often pass through with little or no advance warning. Also, the ambient temperature drops in the late afternoon and evenings tend to be cool.

At the half-way point, Cleetwood Cove, you may want to take a break and enjoy a boat ride on the lake. Tours led by park naturalists leave on the hour and cost $7.25 for adults and $3.75 for children. These 2-hour trips run between the hours of 9 and 3. Make certain to lock your bike, and plan to allow enough time to finish the ride after the boat trip.

Lodging can be found at the Crater Lake Lodge near the Visitor's Center or in one of four camp grounds in the park. Reservations are a must at the lodge and all camp sites are on a first-come, first-served basis.

Eugene Greenway Bike Trail (11 mile loop ride; flat; on marked bike trail)

The City of Eugene, as with many of Oregon's metropolitan areas, has taken great strides to accommodate cyclists. The is partially due to a state-wide 1% gasoline tax reserved for the development of bike trails and routes. Anyone requesting route information at a tourist office or local bike shop will be showered with pamphlets and trail maps. Probably one of the finest maps in any city is the Eugene Bicycle Map, a waterproof vinyl street map that highlights cycling routes throughout the city. It is also marked with isochronal (time) lines so that cyclists can estimate their travel time while planning a ride.

The Greenway Bike Trail follows the banks of the Willamette River, which bisects the city's north/south axis. The land adjacent to the river has been dedicated as a city park and includes the paved bike trail and several pedestrian and bicycle bridges over the water. The Greenway Trail can be accessed from a number of points along the course. Ample parking can be found near the park. A perfect loop occurs between the Greenway Bike Bridge in the north and the Knickerbocker Bicycle Bridge in the south enabling you to return to your starting point without riding back over the same trail.

You will find several stopping points along the way and are never far from shops or lodging. This is also the perfect bicycle route for the business traveler to Eugene. There are a few bike shops near the center of the city that rent bicycles. One piece of advice based on a troublesome experience: if you plan to rent and have a small tool kit with a spare tire at home, take it with you. While on one of these "urban" rides, I experienced a blow-out. The odds were definitely against this happening, yet there I was 5 miles from the nearest repair shop.

Sauvie Island/Portland (12 mile loop, flat route)

This tiny island is situated slightly north and west of the Portland city limit at the junction of the Willamette and Columbia Rivers. It was first settled in 1838 by Laurent Sauve and still retains its rural beauty.

To reach the island by either bicycle or auto, take Highway 30 west from the center of the city. Watch for the Sauvie Island

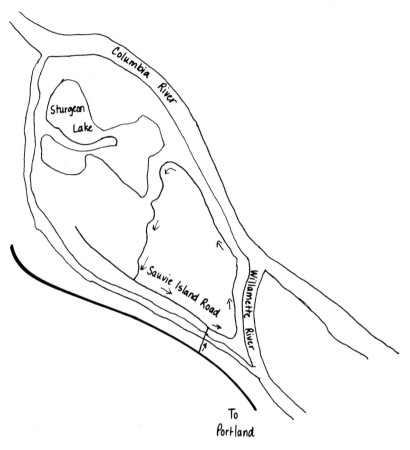

Sauvie Island/Portland—12 miles

turnoff and bridge. You will find convenient parking on a gravel lot to the left after crossing the island bridge to the island. Sauvie Island Road runs east from the parking lot and junctions Gillihan Road, follow this until you reach Reader Road where you will turn left. This will return you to Sauvie Island Road and the bridge.

Portland, as with the City of Eugene, provides several services for cyclists. For $2, you can obtain a waterproof map of the city illustrating several miles of bike routes and trails. They even have a bicycle commuter service, public transportation, and a governmental committee for future development. Bicycles are allowed on most streets, and separate trails have been constructed along many of the interstate freeways. For more information, contact: City of Portland Bicycle and Pedestrian Program, 621 S.W. Alder, Portland, OR 97205. Telephone: (503) 248-4407.

Burke Gilman Bike Trail/Seattle (22 miles round trip to Log Run Park; or 50 miles round trip including Sammamish River Trail; gentle rolling hills and level terrain)

If the cities of Portland and Eugene are the cyclist's mecca of Oregon, then Seattle takes the honors for the northwest. This city is spread out over the rolling hills between Puget Sound on the west and Lake Washington to the east. Seattle has well maintained roads and trails with occasional hills to challenge the recreational rider.

Though many cyclists are attracted to the islands of Puget Sound, they tend to forget the trails along Lake Washington. This body of water is often thought of as an eastern extension of the Pacific Ocean and Puget Sound, but it is actually a large fresh water lake separated by a narrow canal.

The Burke Gilman Bike Trail provides an attractive look at the city and shores of Lake Washington. The trail starts from Gas Works Park, North Lake Way, approximately 1/4 mile east of North 34th Street, then winds through the University of Washington campus and the shores of the lake. It is entirely paved and reserved for bicycle and foot traffic. In several places, birch and pine trees surround the trail giving the im-

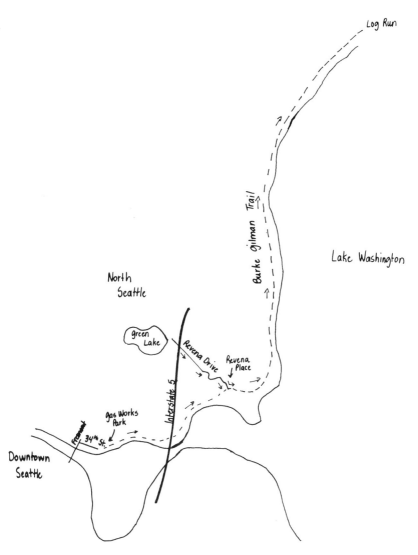

Burke Gilman Trail—Seattle

pression that you are actually riding through the woods.

On the day I road this trail, the weather was cool and a few drops of rain spattered the ground. By the time I reached the northern city limit of Seattle, the sun was shining and there was hardly a cloud in the sky. This is an example of the changeable weather you may experience along any of the northwestern routes during the summer months.

At Log Run Park there are bathrooms, picnic tables, and a place to fill water bottles. If this is the point where you plan to turn around and ride back to the city, you may want to stop and have lunch. Otherwise, press on to the Sammamish Bike Trail. There's a great picnic spot 6 miles away. The Burke Gilman Trail ends in 2 miles, and you will have to ride a short distance along N.E. Bothell Way to reach the start of the Sammamish River Trail. Be careful along here, the road can be narrow and is heavily traveled by cars. Once you reach the Sammamish Trail, you will again be on a separate paved path.

Five miles down the trail, watch for the intersection of N.E. 145th Street. You will want to turn right for a short distance to the St. Michelle Winery. A picnic area is provided along with a wine tasting room. After lunch, continue down the River Trail to its end 4 miles away at Marymoor Park. This large park along the shores of Lake Sammamish offers numerous recreational facilities including a velodrome. You may want to call ahead to find out about the schedule for bicycle races.

There are, of course, many more trails and routes through Washington. A favorite of mine includes a ferry ride from the downtown area to Vashon Island for a day's ride. For more information about these rides and others, check with either the Washington State Department of Transportation (206) 625-4327; or the Seattle Visitors Bureau (206) 447-7273.

GUIDED TOURS

There are two types of guided tours: those sponsored by an organization and hosted for one specific day over a specific course; or those offered by a guide service in much the same style as a pack trip or raft trip.

Fun Rides and Tours

Throughout the Northwestern Region, there are non-profit bicycle clubs that sponsor fun rides each year. One of the best ways to find out about these is through bicycle shops. They usually have bulletin boards where tour information is posted, or they are willing to refer an out-of-town caller to a contact person within the organization. During the summer, it is quite easy to locate a fun ride almost any day of the week in whatever city you might find yourself. These rides follow a marked course and there is no actual guide on the road with you. Most of the sponsoring clubs will provide "sag wagons" (vehicles that patrol the course in case of trouble) and a lunch or snack. In most cases, entry fees range from $15 to $20.

Guided Tours

These trips take three basic forms: self-contained camping, van-supported camping or lodging, and self-contained lodging. Each is usually more than one day in length. Travelers pay a single price that covers all expenses: three meals per day, route maps, professional guides, limited health and accident insurance, tools, first aid kits, etc. The cost can range from $150 to $1600.

There are some distinct advantages to these trips. You are accompanied by a professionally trained guide who will not only take care of cooking meals and minor repairs to bikes, but will point out places of interest along the way. The guides are knowledgeable about weather and road conditions and can alert you in advance about where the hill climbs start and end. This is an important part of making a cycling adventure fun.

Unfortunately, the list of outfitters who provide cycling tours appears to be shrinking. The increased cost of insurance has put many of them out of business. Here is a short listing of outfitters currently offering tours through the Pacific Northwest:

All-Outdoors Adventure Trips, 2151 San Miguel Drive, Walnut Creek, CA 94596; (415) 932-8993. They specialize in tours through the California Mother Lode, Hawaii, and New Zealand. Contact: George Armstrong.

*Riders following a guided tour stop off at one of the wineries in the
Napa Valley.*

Backroads Bicycle Touring, P.O. Box 1626, San Leandro, CA
94577; (415) 895-1783. They offer beginning, intermediate, and
advanced tours for one to ten days through California, the Oregon Coast, and Puget Sound. They also offer luxury weekend
getaways through the California wine country, bicycle rentals,
and lodging at mountain/country inns. The price range of
their tours is as vast as the list they offer; several start at $150
and go up to $1,580. Contact: Tom Hale.

Bikecentennial The Bicycle Travel Association, P.O. Box
8308, Missoula, MT 59807; (406) 721-1776. This is one of the
largest cycling tour operators in the United States. Bikecentennial began as an organization trying to map out a transcontinental route during the celebration of the Bicentennial in
1976. They were so successful that they have remained in business offering several guided trips each year. Aside from their
several routes from either San Francisco, Portland, or Seattle
to the eastern seaboard, they operate numerous local tours. An
especially popular one is the "Northwest Islander" in Seattle,
Washington. This trip begins from the Port of Seattle with a

ferry ride across to an island in Puget Sound. From there, riders spend six days exploring the various islands and spend the nights in comfortable bed-and-breakfast inns. The trip concludes in Victoria, British Columbia, where riders again board a ferry for the return trip to Seattle.

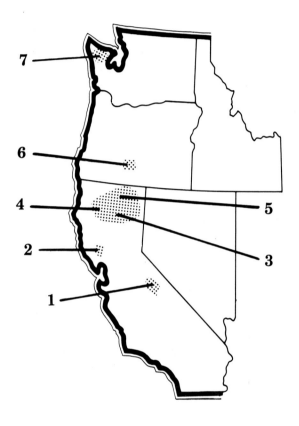

1. *Half Dome Yosemite*
2. *Mount Saint Helena/Napa County CA*
3. *Mount Lassen Peak Trail*
4. *Castle Crags*
5. *Schonchin Butte Lava Beds National Monument*
6. *Mount Scott Crater Lake OR*
7. *Hurricane Ridge Olympic National Park*

4

MOUNTAINEERING

To reach the crest of a high mountain peak and feel the cool westerly breeze as you gaze down at the valleys and hills below sends a thrill up your spine. You seem to be above the clouds as the world passes by you below. And you feel awed in the presence of the mountain.

Mountain climbing is an adventure of inner rewards. There is first the satisfaction of accomplishment. The mountains always held a mystic aura and many early men believed them to be the homes of powerful gods. To reach the summit took strength, determination, and the favor of those gods. Today, a similar feeling persists. The mountain represents a challenge, nature's calling for the careful traveler to join in an adventure.

While on one trip up Half Dome in the Yosemite Valley, I was overwhelmed by the dramatic views of the valley 4800 feet below and the San Joaquin Valley to the west. Seeing that the weather appeared to be holding, I waited there for a while—or at least long enough to enjoy a snack. A few more climbers reached the top, and my snack time was nearing a full hour. Then it was onto dinner, and I set up camp there on the top of the world. As the sun drifted lower, ochre and reddish streaks lit up the remaining sky. The shards of light faded slowly, exposing a night sky that was illuminated by a million tiny stars. I lay back in my mummy bag, my head supported on my pack and studied the lights twinkling above me. I was above the lights and smog from any city and away from any interruption. I began wondering how many of the early men stood on this place and watched the same stars thousands of years ago.

A cascade of water flows over the cliffs and down into Yosemite Valley below. One of many spectacular sights for hikers in this National Park.

They knew nothing of spacecraft or satellite-mounted telescopes or stellar physics, yet they appreciated nature and believed everything held a purpose—even the stars.

In the realm of adventure travel, we often conjure up images of a small group of men dangling from some rocky crag by nylon ropes. The leader wedges a small metal spike into a crack on the granite face, and the team advances another few inches. Much of the adventure in mountaineering comes from the inherent risk of a fall and an almost Freudian thrill of conquest upon reaching the top.

Fortunately for most of us, the mountain peaks have become more accessible to travelers in recent years. There have been advances in climbing gear and techniques, and many State and National Parks have opened access trails to mountain tops. These trails are often overlooked by park visitors. Most people who visit Lava Beds National Monument concentrate on the lava tubes and the site of the Modoc Indian wars, but they overlook Schonchin (Skon-shin) Butte. Or, take the folks who stand by the Visitor's Center at Crater Lake and gaze longingly down at the crystal blue water and the cinder-cone that is Wizard Island. Few of them realize that they can climb up and into the crater of Wizard Island; or that they can ascend to the top of Mount Scott along the park's eastern flank. This peak is the highest point in the park and provides the finest view of Oregon's southern border. Oh, what most of us miss when we fail to look up. But it's hard to see the tree-tops with all the trunks in the way.

In this chapter, we will explore what most of us miss in our parks. We examine what you should do to prepare for a mountain trek or even a half-day walk, and where you can go to climb in the region. Lastly, and for those who get hooked on the mountain high, a list of mountain guides and mountaineering schools has been included.

PREPARING FOR A CLIMB

Most of the climbs described in this chapter require no special equipment and can be accomplished by anyone in moderate physical condition. In most cases, trails are clearly marked and maintained by public agencies.

When preparing for a hike up the side of a mountain, it is important to consider a few details about the terrain and climate. Begin by determining elevation at the start of the trail and at the top. Compare the difference (top elevation minus starting elevation) to the distance in miles that you will actually walk, and you will have a measure of the vertical ascent. Consider two trails: 1) vertical ascent 1,000 feet, distance 2.7 miles; 2) vertical ascent 750 feet, distance 2.7 miles. The first hill will have a steeper climb and, therefore, require greater expenditure of energy. The first trail would be the more difficult.

As you ascend a mountain climatic changes will occur. This will be evident not only in ambient temperature changes but in the type of vegetation you see. At the base may be grassland or deciduous forest (oak or mixed woodland). As altitude increases so does humidity, but the temperature drops. The forest changes from deciduous to coniferous (pine and fir trees).

This zone is referred to as the *montane*. Higher up the mountain's side is the *sub-alpine* zone. Here coniferous trees are adapted to a more rigorous environment—the ambient temperature is even colder. Still further up in the *alpine* zone, trees are replaced by grasses and sedges. And on the very top of a high mountain are perpetual snow and ice.

Obviously, all of these climatic zones are not present on every mountain we climb. They vary according to the elevation and latitudinal location on the planet. A mountain in the Sierra Nevada Range in central California and the other near the Canadian border in the Northern Cascades may have trails that are identical in vertical ascent. But on top of the one in California, a climber may encounter sub-alpine conditions; in northern Washington, by contrast, the climber may need crampons and an ice axe to reach the top.

Here are some of the items you may want to bring with you on any of these hikes. Elevations represent the vertical ascent from the trail head. The trail head is the location of your camp site or automobile, where you will have fresh supplies and shelter.

Zero to 1000 feet

Water

At least one quart per person for an afternoon walk. It is a bad idea to drink water from streams along any of the trails. This is not because of pollution *per se,* but rather a small organism that lives in the water known as Giardia. If you must drink stream water, plan to boil it for more than 5 minutes before using. Also, do not eat snow as a source of fluid. This is a fast way to contract hypothermia if you are already chilled.

First Aid Kit

This should contain the basic supplies along with a snake bite and bee sting kit. This is not much of a problem in the West, but a few cases occur each year on hillsides.

Clothing

This is the most important factor. Shirts should be layered with a cotton tee shirt, and natural fiber outer shirt. Pants should be of a stretch material, allowing comfortable movement. Socks should be thick enough to protect against blisters and should cushion the feet. You will want a sweater, preferably 100% natural fiber.

Shoes

You should have a good pair of hiking boots. This does not mean you need to run right out and buy the most expensive pair of Swiss climbing boots! There are several comfortable light weight boots on the market. They can be nylon or leather but should offer arch and ankle support.

1000 to 1500 feet

Everything on the preceding list, plus:

Food

This does not mean a full 5-course meal of dehydrated trail food and the equipment for cooking it. But you will need a snack: fresh fruit, mixed nuts, a few pieces of hard candy. Avoid eating too much salt and don't take in alcoholic beverages.

Wind Breaker

This adds another layer of clothing over the sweater in case you encounter moisture.

Hat

This provides protection from the sun and harmful ultraviolet light.

Sun Screen

It is much easier to get a bad sunburn at higher elevations. The air is thinner and more ultraviolet light reaches the ground.

1500 feet and above

Everything on the preceding lists, plus:

Additional Water

Due to the increased length of this hike, plan to carry more water.

Clothing for Wet Weather

Weather conditions can change, and if you enter an alpine zone, it may be foggy or snowing. Gaiters keep pant legs and socks dry. Also include rain gear, a wool knit cap, and possibly a parka.

Eye Protection

If an alpine zone is to be encountered, plan on bringing a pair of sunglasses. The reflection off snow and ice can cause "snow blindness" and burns. This can result in a very painful condition after the climb. You usually don't know you have been burned until a few hours later.

Along with equipment planning, consider what action may be necessary if conditions should change. The weather in a mountainous area is always subject to *sudden* change. Even a gust of wind at lower elevations can affect a hiker by causing temperatures to drop. This is known as windchill. On a calm day where the air temperature is 40°, if a 25-mile-per-hour wind comes up the temperature you feel drops to 15°. Should this or a sudden thunder storm happen when you're halfway up a hillside, you will need to have a plan and equipment to deal with it.

ON THE TRAIL

After deciding what to carry in your pack, give some thought to safety on the trail. The last main topic in planning for any hike whether it be a mountain climb or just a walk in the woods is safety. Follow these precautions:

1) File a written copy of your trip plan with a friend or loved one not going on the hike. This should include departure location, departure time, route, location of summit, return route, approximate time starting return, ending location, and approximate ending time.

2) Travel with a partner. Ideally, the group should be made up of at least three people. This way if a person is hurt, one member can help administer first aid while the other goes for help.

3) When traveling as a group, don't split up. This should be obvious, yet it remains one of the major causes of problems.

4) Watch for loose rocks and gravel on the trail. Unsure footing can result in a fall or drop rocks on hikers below.

Thunderstorms are frequent in the alpine country of the Northwest. They are commonplace in the higher elevations and usually occur in the mid- to late-afternoon. Aside from the accompanying rain, you will have to deal with lightning. The possibility of being struck by lightning while on a high peak during a thunderstorm is a real threat. Tragedy has struck almost every year at some of the more popular peaks when hikers don't heed lightning warnings. If you are caught in a sudden thunderstorm, take immediate action to keep from getting soaked by the rain or targeted by lightning. Avoid open clearings, lone trees, tall power poles, or mountain tops. Take cover in a forest, away from the tallest trees, or in a cave. Should you find yourself in an open area without accessible cover the U.S. Forest Service recommends you put insulating material (poncho or foam pad) on a small rock and sit on it.

While on a hike up Schonchin Butte with my 5-year-old daughter, we arrived at the fire lookout just as a thunderstorm approached from the southwest. The trail up was on the opposite side of the mountain, and we were completely unaware of the storm until we reached the top. The ranger took us into the lookout where he was preparing for the lightning. As he took a small rectangular stool out that had glass insulators on the legs, he related a story from the prior day. Another couple arrived just as a storm was approaching. He instructed them to remove any metal objects they were wearing, while he locked the door. Then, they stood atop the stool facing one another. As the storm approached, there was a strong wind and the station was pelted by hail and rain. The static electricity discharged by the cloud caused their hair to rise and a tingling sensation crawled over their skin. Outside, the four ground wires at each corner of the lookout began humming and crackling, and then came the explosion of thunder as the station was hit by lightning.

On this day, the storm passed without incident and the ranger stored the small stool away and re-opened the station. It was business as usual, and all was well. My daughter and I were slightly dazed by the experience, but the ranger explained that it was a common occurrence on the mountain top. I can just imagine what that experience would have been like had there not been a lookout post. About 20 minutes passed from the time we first saw the storm until the station was re-opened.

While on the trail, remember your relationship to the mountain and the wilderness you're passing through. Be aware of your surroundings as far as both plants and animals are concerned and the effect your presence has on them. The National Park Service reminds us to enjoy the parks but remember to feed nothing, leave nothing, and take nothing. In this way we can insure the preservation of our natural resources for the next traveler, and possibly ourselves on a subsequent visit.

A very serious threat to the forest environment comes from cigarette butts. Discarded filters contain a high concentration of tar and nicotine and are not biodegradable. This combination can be a source of toxins to wildlife and plants. If you smoke and plan to take a mountain hike, please be careful with fire. And take the remains out with you when you leave.

There is one final comment that is very important to the preservation of our wilderness areas. Most of the trips along the mountains of the Northwest are taken along publicly maintained trails. It cannot be emphasized enough that hikers should STAY ON THE MARKED TRAILS. Even a few people taking short-cuts when a trail makes a steep switch-back along a slope or making their own detour can cause major damage to surface vegetation. During a rain storm, soil may erode from the damaged area and flow down the hillside to cause greater problems for the delicate forest ecosystem. A naturalist/ranger at the Olympic National Park in Washington estimated that as few as ten people could trigger this erosive cycle. The problem is almost as serious as an uncontrolled fire.

Those of you who decide to take the trail up the side of Mount Saint Helena in the Northern Napa Valley, California will get several opportunities to see these damaged areas. Within the first mile of the walk, I counted nine areas where vegetation had washed away because of people taking short-cuts. Many parks may close trails to allow the forest to recover from this type of overuse. Crews of rangers will often attempt to repair the damaged areas by shoring up the sides of trails with heavy lumber. Therefore, you may find on a day when you expected to take one of the trails listed here that the park service has closed it. Give some thought as to the reasons. And, if you see anyone taking a short-cut, express your displeasure and advise a ranger should you get a license number or name.

LIGHT MOUNTAINEERING TOURS

Half Dome/Yosemite (9 miles one-way; 4,800 feet vertical)

At the end of the Half Dome Trail is one of the most spectacular views from any vista. From here you can gaze out over the other peaks and down to the valley floor. The sheer north face of this rock makes the grand view possible.

To reach the trail head of the Half Dome Trail, you will have to walk 6.2 miles along the first portion of the John Muir Trail. The start of the trail is at Happy Isle along the southwestern side of the Yosemite VAlley, where the Merced River flows in. This is the last location for water bottles and can-

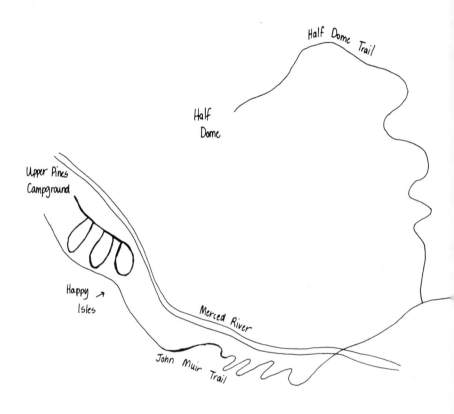

Half Dome Yosemite—9 miles, 4800 ft vertical

Half Dome appears as a formidable obstacle, yet can be climbed by just about anyone using a special ladder set up during the summer season.

teens to be filled. From this point forward, the trail markers denote several trail names; follow the signs to Half Dome. Starting on the Nevada Falls trail, the route follows along the left bank of the Merced River.

Just above Nevada Falls, the route joins with the Merced Lake trail. Turning here and following this trail, you will enter Little Yosemite Valley. This unspoiled meadow makes a nice stopping point for a short break. Climbing out of the valley, you will be greeted by views of Half Dome's south face. The rock looks massive from this vista. Its sheer granite walls reflecting the morning sun, the dome stands as a reminder of the massive forces that shaped the valley floors. To some, it resembles a fortress built high on a promontory, protecting and dominating the realm at its feet. In a short while, you will be higher than the dome itself.

The Merced Lake Trail continues climbing to the junction of the Half Dome Trail at an elevation of 7,000 feet. Here you will turn and make the final walk to the base of the rock. The trail makes many tight switch-back turns as it winds up to the 8,000-foot level. Along the side of the dome, the National Park Service has erected a cable ladder to allow visitors to climb on top of the rock.

Many visitors may want to take alternate routes to the top from this point. If you opt not to use the cable ladder you will need special rock climbing equipment, training, and experience. If you want to attempt this, contact the Yosemite Mountaineering School listed in the following section. For this climb, it is extremely important to note weather conditions before and during the hike to the mountain. Half Dome is nearly always struck by lightning during a thunderstorm. DO NOT GO UP if there is even a threat of a storm. This has led to several fatalities in the past.

Lodging can be found in the Yosemite Valley. The Curry Company operates the Yosemite and Wawona lodges all year and the park service has several camp grounds in the area. Reservations should be made four to eight weeks in advance of a trip into the valley. This is one of the few National Parks where campsites can also be reserved. You can call any Ticketron outlet or the Yosemite Park (209) 372-1000 for information.

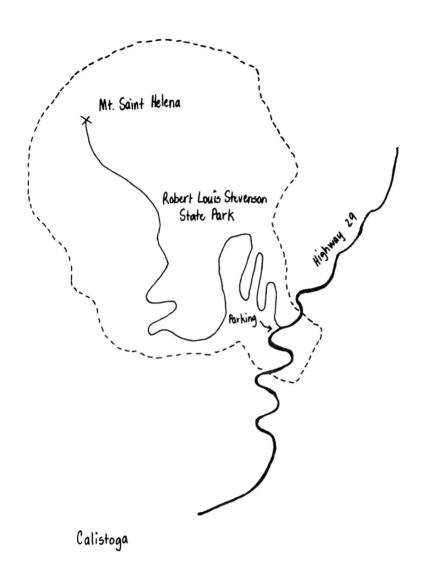

Mt. Saint Helena

Robert Louis Stevenson
State Park

Highway 29

Parking

Calistoga

Mount St. Helena—5 miles one way, 950 ft vertical

Mount Saint Helena/Napa County, California
(5 miles one way, 950 feet vertical)

This excellent walk was first pointed out to me by the innkeepers of Foothill House in Calistoga, California. They are blessed with a beautiful view of the mountain from their balconies. The trail offers not only fabulous vistas of the valley but provides an excellent escape from the usual summer heat.

Mount Saint Helena sits regally at the northern tip of the famed Napa Valley. All of the lower ridges and peaks seem to funnel in at this point and culminate in the steep slopes of this volcanic mountain. It towers a few thousand feet above any of the other surrounding hills and dominates the landscape as you drive north on Highway 29.

The trail starts from the Robert Lewis Stevenson State Park off of State Highway 29. Locating the trail head is a challenge in itself. There are no resident rangers in this park, no dramatic entrances or visitor's information stands. Heading north out of Calistoga, Highway 29 starts a steep and winding ascent of the mountain into the State Park. Watch for a large sign that says you are entering the park. Slow down if possible and watch for the first gravel turnout on the left side of the road. Along the far side of the turnout, a few wood steps lead up into the forest. This is the trail head.

Park your vehicle in the turnout well off the main road. There are several curves in Highway 29 in this area and traffic moves near the speed limit so exercise caution when getting out of the car. Remember to lock your car and keep all valuables out of sight.

The climb of the mountain begins with a gentle grade to the Robert Lewis Stevenson monument (1 mile). This is an excellent place to pause for awhile and take in the surroundings. It was in this grove that he honeymooned with his bride and wrote *Silverado Squatters*.

After leaving the monument, the trail steepens and you enter a chaparral and mixed woodland. There are several sharp turns and areas where the grade will make walking just difficult enough to remind you that you're climbing a mountain. On the top, the views stretch nearly to the Pacific Ocean and to the large lakes in the northeast. It is time to spread the blanket and open the picnic basket. Now where is that bottle of sparkling water?

This trek is best taken in the mid-morning and early afternoon. Remember it is a 10-mile round-trip walk that will take the better part of the day. There is no water anywhere along the route or in the park, so be sure to prepare a canteen before leaving Calistoga.

Lodging can be found in the town of Calistoga. There are several fine bed-and-breakfast inns, of which Foothill House, Brannan Cottage, and the Mountain View Hotel are the best. Any one of these three would be fine for climbers of the mountain, but Foothill House heads the list. This inn consists of only four attractive suites and two innkeepers who will take close care of you.

After leaving the mountain, climbers may experience a degree of muscle soreness. For this, the town of Calistoga and its mineral baths are famous. Since the turn of the century, people have traveled here to soak in the natural springs. Dr. Wilkinson's, one of the older European-style spas, offers complete treatments that include a supervised mud bath, mineral bath, steam, and full massage. After one of his two-and-a-half-hour treatments, you will be ready for dinner and a restful evening remembering your trek up Mount Saint Helena in the California wine country.

Mount Lassen Peak Trail (2.5 miles one way; 1945 feet vertical)

This remains one of the most remarkable climbs in Northern California. Mount Lassen provides a glimpse into the realm of active volcanoes and is probably very similar to how Mount Saint Helens may have appeared years prior to its eruption. On rare occasions, steam spurts from the top of this volcano, but that is not the only sign of activity in the area. Mount Lassen is surrounded by bubbling mudpots, steam vents and hot springs—all evidence of current activity.

State Highway 89 enters Lassen National Park from the north and south. The road winds past the several volcanic sites in the park where visitors can stop and make their own examinations. One of the more popular areas along this route is

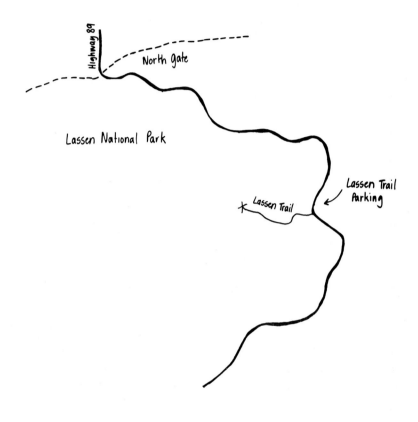

Mount Lassen Peak Trail—2.5 miles one way, 1945 ft vertical

Bumpass Hell. A brief 1.3-mile trail leads down from the highway. It was named for an early hunter who mistakenly stepped into one of the boiling pools.

From either entrance, the highway winds up the side of the mountain to a large parking area. With the exception of very dry seasons, snow usually remains on the ground at the parking area (elevation 8512 feet). From here, climbers cross the highway to the trail. Snow may be encountered on any portion of the trail, depending on seasonal conditions. No special equipment is required aside from a sturdy pair of walking shoes and a hooded jacket. It is usually cold on the top. On my last trip up, I found that a pair of nylon gaiters helped keep my lower legs dry and warm. Be forewarned that this entire trek is at high altitudes. If you are not used to these conditions, take the trail slowly and don't be afraid to make frequent rest stops. You will want to avoid sitting in the snow no matter how hot you may feel from your efforts. The danger of hypothermia is real. Also, avoid eating snow in place of water. You will want to fill a canteen at one of the visitor's centers or rest areas along the highway.

From the top of Mount Lassen, you will be rewarded with a marvelous view. To the west: the fertile Sacramento Valley and Coastal Mountains beyond; several crystal blue lakes lie scattered between the smaller volcanic peaks in almost every other direction. And at your feet is the gaping crater of the mountain. This is one of the highest peaks that is easily accessible for travelers. Most of the other mountains over 10,000 feet require the aid of trained guides to negotiate their slopes.

Castle Crags (2.7 miles one way; 2,241 feet vertical)

This is one of the more challenging climbs in the Northwest. The crags and the State Park are often passed up by visitors because of their close proximity to the Interstate 5 freeway. "Such is life," one climber commented to me. "They don't realize what they're missing."

Most travelers along the interstate pause to look at the truly castle-like spires of the crags. Some may even pause to snap a photo. They crane their necks to study the sheer walls rising from a green forested hillside. Up to this point, the majority of

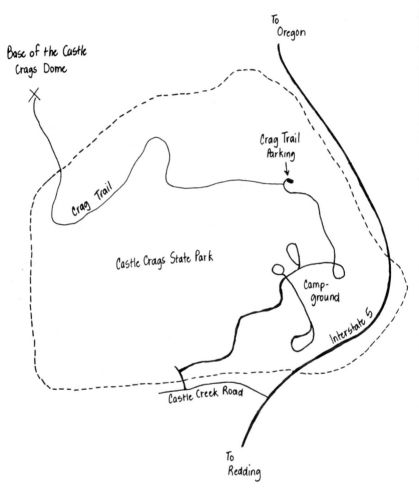

Base of the Castle
Crags Dome

To
Oregon

Crag Trail
Parking

Crag Trail

Castle Crags State Park

Camp-
ground

Interstate 5

Castle Creek Road

To
Redding

Castle Crags—2.7 miles one way, 2241 vertical

*Castle Crags offers a rewarding climb up a trail
seemingly designed for mountain goats.*

the mountains were rolling foothills and a few tree-lined ridges. Certainly nothing like the 2–300-foot walls of a natural fortress that they now encounter.

Unlike Yosemite's Half Dome, the castle does not appear as though a single rock, but rather a masterpiece of architectural fortification—enough to make a medieval king's mouth water. From a distance, one finds it hard to believe that this was not constructed by man.

For the fortunate who take a moment to wander into Castle Crags State Park, they are afforded a view from a specially constructed vista point. This is just a short drive up a narrow, one-lane road from the park's entrance. At the parking lot, you walk up a short trail to the lookout. To the west is Castle Crags, and between the trees further to the north rises the glacier-covered Mount Shasta. On a clear day, a camera equipped with a wide angle lens and positioned just right can capture the images of both of these northern giants.

The start of the Crag Trail junctions the vista point road just before the parking area. It is clearly marked by a large sign. The path to the base of the Crag dome is well maintained up to the border of the State Park. Although the park and the peak share the same name, they are not one and the same. The actual mountain is in U.S. Forest Service land. For the sake of the hiker, this does not really affect things. The trail is improved all the way to the base of the dome. Anyone wishing to go further up should be equipped and trained for a difficult rock climb. A mountain guide is listed at the end of this chapter who can provide more information.

It is satisfying enough to stand at the foot of the dome and realize that the castle loses nothing close up. Also, from this point, you are afforded a view of the Sacramento River gorge and an entirely fresh perspective of Shasta. When contemplating a climb up to Castle Crags, you should be prepared with extra water and good climbing shoes. The first portion of the trail is very mild, but you can imagine what the remainder is like as you climb 2,000 feet higher. This is a fun hike, and because of its demanding terrain, not heavily traveled. Take a moment now and again to watch for wildlife. The Autumn coloring can be quite dramatic in this section of the Southern Cascades and makes this an excellent Fall excursion.

The trail head up to the Castle Dome. Easy enough at first, until it starts curving upward.

A few suggestions are in order should you think about taking this hill. Prior to heading up the trail, it is a good idea to check in with the ranger station and let them know you're taking the trail. Even though the trail is much shorter than many of the others in this book, give yourself the better part of a full day to complete the hike. Lastly, the rangers in the park do not recommend that persons in poor physical condition or with high blood pressure attempt the climb.

Lodging can be found in nearby Dunsmuir or, if you're up to camping, consider the State Park. If you don't feel comfortable tackling the trail to the top, consider taking the Indian Creek Nature Trail or the River Trail. Both are within the park and offer gentler hikes through equally beautiful country. Railroad Park, one of the more unusual and attractive motels, is just north of Castle Crags along Interstate 5. This inn boasts a selection of restored cabooses and railroad cars that have been converted into attractive suites. Their restaurant provides an excellent place to celebrate your return from the mountain as the setting sunlight illuminates the last spires and darkness settles on the valley.

Schonchin Butte/Lava Beds National Monument
(.75 mile one-way; 476 feet vertical)

This recent cinder cone volcano was named after the Modoc Indian Chief who controlled the tribe during the settlement of the white man in the Tule Lake area. The mountain stands alone by the south edge of the lava beds and seems to watch over the area, much as the old chief might have. The National Park Service erected a fire lookout station at the very top and improved a trail up the southeast face.

This is one of the side trips in Lava Beds that is often missed by many visitors. As you stand at the base of this imposing cinder cone, its flanks appear very steep and impassable. Also this mountain, much like its relatives, appears to be made up of tiny stones. Your perception is that you might sink in up to your knees if you walked on it. The other side of the mountain, however, is not only sheltered from the westerly winds as well as from the view of passers-by, but is less steep and is covered with vegetation.

Visitors to the park are encouraged to climb Schonchin Butte. The fire lookout at the very top is manned every day during the summer season. The rectangular structure is perched atop a huge basalt lava plug that was forced through the crater during the last eruption. On a clear day, you can see from Mount Maclaughlin in the north to Glass Mountain in the south, from Shasta in the west on to the plains of Nevada in the east.

The climb is relatively easy. My five-year-old daughter and I climbed the hill in a little over half an hour. And as we approached the mountain top, the ranger was standing out on the deck waiting to greet us. He demonstrated the equipment inside of the lookout for us and carefully pointed out each of the geological features of the Butte.

Lava Beds National Monument is well known for its many caves (see cave exploring chapter) and lava flows. This is a land of stark beauty, where the slopes of the eastern Cascades drop off into a great basin. This is also the home for many wild

Approaching the fire lookout on top of Schonchin Butte.

birds and animals. Soon after the climb, as we drove slowly around the base of the mountain back to the highway, we observed a pair of badgers, and watched as a red tailed hawk swooped down to grab a rodent.

The park is located in California's northeastern corner. From Redding, along Interstate Highway 5, take State Highway 299 east to the town of Bieber. Watch for Lookout Road (the Tule Lake turn off). Take this north to Highway 139. Again, turn north (left) and proceed along the northern boundary of the Modoc National Forest to County Road 97. Turn left. From here, just follow the signs to Lava Beds. If you're heading into or out of Oregon, Lava Beds makes a great stopover. All of the northbound roads lead to the city of Klamath Falls, OR.

One important word of advice. There are no gas stations or grocery stores in this very large park so make sure to stock up and fill the tank before entering. The nearest lodging is in the town of Tule Lake to the north. The park provides 40 attractive campsites on a first-come-first-served basis. Plan to arrive in the morning on a weekday and you will more than likely get a campsite without problems.

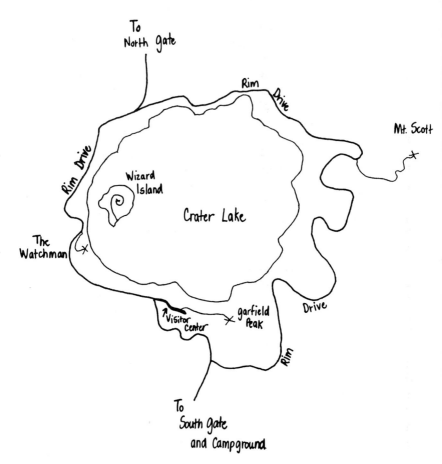

Mount Scott—2.5 miles, 976 ft vertical

Mount Scott/Crater Lake, Oregon (2.5 miles; 976 feet vertical)

Ten thousand years ago, Mount Mazama stood 12,000 feet high on the site that is now Crater Lake. Indian legends tell of a fiery conflict between two gods. In the end, one god dropped the mountain onto the other in proclamation of his victory. But the conflict was not over. The underworld god continued to struggle, so it was necessary to fill the crater with water.

Geologists tell us a slightly different story about the origin of the Crater Lake caldera, but the net result was the creation of a truly magnificent monument. The lake is the deepest in the continental United States and has the highest clarity. These two factors give the water a unique azure blue color that appears to come from an artist's palette.

Mount Scott stands tall along the park's eastern border. It is the highest point in the area and provides a foundation for a fire lookout station. From its peak, you're offered views of the dense Oregon forests and of the lake itself. This is a good place for photographers who want to capture an image of the entire lake. Also, if you take this trail early enough in the morning, you may catch a glimpse of the rare Peregrine Falcon and several species of mammals, including the Yellow-Bellied Marmot.

The trail leaves the Rim Road near Cloud Cap. Unfortunately, this is located almost three quarters of the way around the rim of Crater Lake along a one-way road so be sure to allow enough time for the drive. The climb itself maintains a steep pace up to the top of the ridge. The altitude at the trail head is already over 8,000 feet. This may present problems for people not in fairly good physical condition or those with high blood pressure.

I found a walking staff helpful in the climb. I was able to rest on it and use it for extra balance on the steeper sections. At the top, I set it down along with my day pack and took in the beautiful view. For a moment, it was as though I had arrived in another world. The bright blue lake below seemed vastly different. Its blueness offered a stark contrast to the rock walls of the caldera, and the scene was framed by the deep green forests that surround the mountain.

Lodging is available during the summer season at the Crater Lake Lodge. There are 198 sites in the Mazama Campground along the southern side of the park. As with Lava Beds, the campsites are full most evenings and on weekends. You should plan on arriving by the early afternoon in order to claim a good site. A grocery store, restaurants, and a gas station can be found near the Visitor's Center.

The trip up Mount Scott is one not to be missed. It will be very obvious why this park is one of the most popular in the West and attracts large crowds. For this reason, Mount Scott provides an especially pleasant getaway. You can count on seeing hardly a soul on this trail.

There are three more mountain tops located within Crater Lake that are relatively easy climbs:

The Watchman is a butte right on the shore of the lake along the western side. During the early years of the park, this lookout post was used to observe boats on the lake while they performed scientific experiments. The trail is 0.8 miles long and leaves from a parking area off of Rim Drive. This is one of the more popular hills to climb in the park because of its proximity to both the lake and Rim Drive. Unfortunately, the heavy foot traffic has taken its toll on the trail and environment. While I was visiting the park, the rangers had just closed the trail for the season to allow the area to recover. This is an unfortunate testament to the damage caused when people take short-cuts on trails.

Garfield Peak is located southwest of the Visitor's Center. This 2.7 mile trail leaves from the Crater Lake Lodge and takes you through thick forests. As you walk on this one, be especially watchful for wildlife. You may want to time this walk so that your return is in the late afternoon. Many animals become more active during this time as they begin searching for food.

From the top of Garfield Peak, you will get another perspective of the lake and an unobstructed view of Klamath Falls and the California border to the south. Be sure to take your camera and extra water on this trek.

Wizard Island rises up from the surface of Crater Lake. This cinder cone grew during an eruption that finally sealed the caldera and allowed it to fill with water. The island can be

Wizard Island, aptly named by the Indians who witnessed the formation of the lake.

reached by one of the several tour boats leaving from Cleetwood Cove. You will have to take the earlier boats if you plan to hike to the top of this cinder cone. The first boat leaves Cleetwood at 9:00 A.M. and the last leaves the island at 3:00 P.M.

One of the favorite pastimes of visitors to Wizard Island is to walk down into the crater. Here there is usually a snow field that provides a great escape from summer heat and a few hours of fun. No camping or fires are allowed on the island. You will want to pack in a lunch and plenty of water, as none are available after leaving Cleetwood Cove.

Hurricane Ridge/Olympic National Park

This is the starting point for several attractive walks through one portion of a very large park. Olympic National Park was established to preserve the Roosevelt Elk. This was accomplished along with a great deal more. The park provides one of the finest recreational escapes for hikers and travelers in the

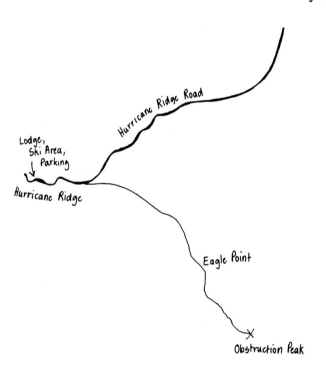

Hurricane Ridge/Obstruction Peak—8 miles, 970 ft vertical

Northwest. Olympic National Park is located along the northern tip of the Olympic Peninsula; to the north is Vancouver Island, Canada, and to the east is Puget Sound and metropolitan Seattle.

One of the favorite climbs is up to Hurricane Hill. This starts from the Hurricane Ridge Lodge along a well marked nature trail. The climbs are gentle and the views dramatic. On a clear day as you approach the top, you can make out the distant shores of Vancouver Island and the City of Victoria. Then, once you clear the tree tops, you can see the islands in

From Hurricane Ridge: the view of the Straits of Juan de Fuca, with Canada in the distance.

Puget Sound, Mount Rainier, and Mount Baker in the Northern Cascades National Park.

While standing on Hurricane Hill, photographing the distant vistas, my five-year-old tugged on my pants, and proclaimed that she saw a bear. Dad didn't believe her at first and continued to concentrate on focusing my zoom lens. But then she became even more excited and insisted that I look. Well, she was right. In the valley along the slopes of Mount Angeles was a single black bear. The large creature lumbered along and, just as I aimed the camera, disappeared into the woods. On the way down, we observed a single mule deer not forty feet from us, resting in the shade of a large mountain hemlock tree.

From Hurricane Ridge, one of the more popular trails follows an unpaved fire road along the ridge to Obstruction Point. This 8-mile (one-way) climb leads you along the crest of the ridge. the vertical is approximately 970 feet, so the trail negotiates a gentle grade. The finest views of Mount Olympus and

Puget Sound await at the end. You can obtain permission to camp at the top of Obstruction Point depending upon the weather and potential fire conditions. Otherwise, plan on taking this trail in the early morning and enjoy a picnic lunch on the top. Be on the lookout for wildlife on the way. I like to take along a bird and tree guide when taking climbs like this one. There are plenty of places to stop and watch for animal life, and it is especially fun to be able to make a rare sighting in the wild.

Lodging can be found in the city of Port Angeles, just north of the park. If you enjoy camping, I strongly recommend the Heart of the Hills campground in the park. Each site has been carefully placed within a large grove of cedar and redwoods. It is a very peaceful and tranquil area. Also in the park, a few miles further west along U.S. 101, is the Sol Duc resort. Lodging and camping can be found near the natural hot springs. After a climb along Hurricane Ridge, there's nothing like a dip in the springs to relax.

MOUNTAINEERING SCHOOLS AND GUIDES

Many of the major peaks in the Northwestern Region can be climbed with the aid of special equipment, training, or a guide. Some of the mountains, like Shasta, don't require much in the way of training but a guide service is strongly recommended.

In this section, a sampling of mountaineering schools and guide services are listed. This is not a complete list by any stretch of the imagination. There are guides available that specialize in more than just climbing a mountain. For instance, many offer to lead you over steep ridges to remote lakes for rainbow trout; others lead hunting trips. These types of guides have not been included in this text. For information regarding sport guides, contact the U.S. Forest Service Ranger Station in the area you wish to visit. They usually have a complete list of the licensed guides in their jurisdictions.

Most mountaineering schools offer basic seminars in rock climbing, with follow-up advanced classes in rock and ice

Mount Shasta, one of the easier mountains to climb with the aid of a guide and special equipment. A good mountain to start on for those interested in technical climbing.

climbing. Nearly all of the schools provide a guide service for graduates and experienced climbers. When selecting a school, interview their representative. Try to determine what their goal is in operating the school; how they plan to achieve the goal; what their technique of instruction is; what their instructors are like; and, how much it costs. Finally, determine what their safety record is like. Have they experienced a lot of problems? And, how long have they been in business? Most high quality guide services and mountaineering schools will not object to answering any of these questions. Should they become too defensive, though, look elsewhere.

There are several reasons people go to mountaineering school. For many, it is not a desire to someday climb Mount Everest. Most just want to learn some basic techniques to help them in recreational treks. As with many adventure trips, your reason could be just for the experience of it. "It's something I've always wanted to do," one young lady explained as she graduated from the Yosemite Mountaineering School.

Yosemite Mountaineering School: Bruce Brossman, Director; Yosemite National Park, CA 95389; (209) 372-1244. Courses: Basic rock climbing; Intermediate Rock II; Intermediate Rock III; Summer Snow Climbing; Alpencraft; Snow and Ice; Alpine Climbing.

Palisade School of Mountaineering: John Fischer, Director; P.O. Box 694, Bishop, CA 93514; (619) 873-5037. Courses: Basic Mountaineering; Basic Rock Climbing; Ice Climbing; Advanced Mountaineering; Mountain Medicine.

Mount Whitney Guide Service and Sierra Nevada School of Mountaineering: David Kruger, Director; P.O. Box 659, Lone Pine, CA 93545; (619) 876-4500. Courses: 4-day General Mountaineering Seminar; 4-day East Face Seminar; 4-day Peak Bagging Seminar (for previously trained and experienced individuals).

Timberline Mountain Guides: P.O. Box 464, Terrebonne, OR 97760; (503) 548-1888. They specialize in climbing seminars and trips up Mount Hood and Smith Rock. Courses: Rock Climbing; Ice Climbing; Mountaineering; Alpine Climbing; Ski Mountaineering; Winter Climbing; Avalanche Seminars.

Shasta Mountain Guides: 1938 Hill Road, Mount Shasta City, CA 96067; (916) 926-3117. Mike Zanger, owner, leads 1- and 2-day treks up Mount Shasta. This is a great trip for a first-time climber.

Ranier Mountaineering: (summer) Paradise, WA 98398; (206) 569-2227; (winter) 201 St. Helens aVe., Tacoma, WA 98402; (206) 627-6242. They specialize in climbs of the most glaciated volcanic peak in the United States, Mount Rainier. Courses: 1-day Basic Climbing School; Snow and Ice Climbing; Expedition Climbing; 2-day Ice Climbing; Crevasse Rescue School; Mountain Medicine.

Leavenworth Alpine Guides: P.O. Box 699, Leavenworth, WA 98826; (509) 548-4729. Courses: 1/2-day Basic Rock Course; Basic Rock Climbing; Intermediate Rock Course; Advanced Rock Course; Basic Mountaineering; Intermediate Mountaineering; Canadian Rockies Ice Course; Mountain Medicine; Avalanche Seminars; Waterfall Ice; Ski Mountaineering.

Elephant's Perch Mountain Specialists: Bob Rosso, Proprietor; P.O. Box 178, Ketchum, ID 83340; (208) 726-3497. This is an outfitter of mountaineering equipment. On several occasions they have held seminars on basic and advanced mountain climbing. The city of Ketchum is close to the Sawtooth Mountains, which offer challenging peaks for all mountain climbing enthusiasts. As for guide services, this outfitter will refer clients to specialists.

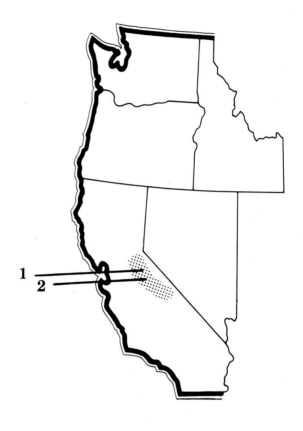

1. *Gold Prospecting Expeditions*
2. *Matelot Gulch Mining Co.*

5

GOLD
COUNTRY

As spring comes and the days grow longer, the rolling hills and rustic towns of the California Mother Lode attract the eye of the traveler. The gold country is rich in silent monuments which serve as reminders of the region's colorful past. Museums, historic parks, and quaint old towns tell of the men who swarmed the hills in search of treasure. James Marshall's discovery of gold in 1848 touched off one of the largest westward movements in history.

In the sixteen years that followed Marshall's discovery, massive mining operations were undertaken. Time and time again every river and creek was thoroughly scoured. Miners followed rough deposits of ore from the streams and tunneled into the hills, extracting gold from quartz lode veins. The work was hard and the days long. As gold pockets in streams dwindled, miners who had once been alone and free-spirited took jobs in the large mines.

The last commercial mining operation started during the gold rush didn't shut down until 1968. From 1848 until then, a total of 106,000,000 troy ounces of fine gold had been extracted. The price of gold was approximately $35 per ounce, and indications were that this would remain stable. And, due to costly mining methods, commercial operations were no longer cost-effective. A sign of the times was evident when the U.S. Treasury Department suspended all purchases of newly mined gold in 1968. Many believed that was the end of an era. Or was it?

Who would have ever imagined that gold prices would top $800 per ounce, as they did on January 16, 1980? And, who

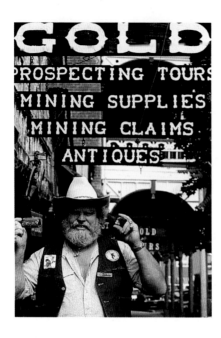

You might be able to pan enough to pay for your vacation.

could believe that a few lucky tourists on vacation might find enough gold to pay for part, if not all, of their vacation? An amateur miner, with no special connections, can get roughly 80% of the market price for his gold. However, some jewelers might pay much more for a nugget.

Aside from the value of gold itself, mining offers several side benefits. Consider that placer gold mining (searching for surface gold in creeks and streams by panning or dredging) is good exercise and a way to get away from it all. After battling inner-urban life day in and day out, a gold mining trip is like traveling back in time. Apart from the more modern methods of extracting ore, you live the life of a forty-niner: sleeping under a carpet of stars; enjoying hearty mining camp chow; and, if you're lucky, seeing "color" in your pan.

NEW TOOLS FOR OLD TECHNIQUES

The basic techniques for locating gold have not changed since the early days of the gold rush in California. Gold can be found in the form of flower-like dust, flakes or, if you really hit the jackpot, nuggets.

To search successfully for the most coveted metal in the world, you should understand a few basic principles about where the stuff comes from. Gold deposits in the West were formed during the Jurassic period—the era of the dinosaurs. As a result of erosive forces later in the Cretaceous period, the deposits appeared closer to the surface. As weather and the movement of the continents continued, gold veins eroded and small fragments tumbled downward into streams and rivers. Being one of the heavier elements in the water, the deposits traveled slowly and usually in a straight line as the force of the water worked against them. When the stream changed course or crested a boulder, the gold would lodge on the leeward side of a rock or become entombed in a sand bar. These deposits in stream beds or along hillsides are called placer deposits. When the gold is still a part of the vein, it is referred to as a lode deposit.

When James Marshall touched off the famous gold rush in the West, the miners used a variety of placer mining techniques. They used pans, shakers, and sluice boxes to separate the lighter-weight dirt and rocks from the gold. It was back-breaking work, but they were driven by a single desire: to trace the placer gold back to its origin at the lode and strike it rich. Obviously, this happened to only a few people who were lucky enough to be in the right place at the right time, so to speak.

It is commonly believed that no rock or stone has been untouched in the Sierra foothills by the forty-niners and, therefore, all of the gold has been removed. Well, this is not the case. A member of the U.S. Department of the Interior Geological Survey estimated that one-third of the placer gold deposits were completely missed by the forty-niners during hydraulic mining. This was a devastating process that tore apart the river banks and hillsides in order to wash heavy gold deposits down. It is also estimated that 20% of the placer gold found today was present during the California gold rush. The rest is from recent erosion over the last 100 years!

Today's miners use more sophisticated equipment than what was available to the forty-niners. Although the old-staple mining pan remains, a few high-tech modifications have been made. For one, the pans are constructed out of light-weight plastic and are easily transported. They are already a dark color and are ready to use. The old metal pans had to be burned in order to darken them so the gold would appear. Also, small riffles similar to those found in a sluice box have been added on one side of the pan. This allows you to carefully wash smaller particles with greater precision.

Along with the pan, small dredges have been constructed to allow the recreational miner to access the deeper, more concealed sections of a stream bed. Particles of sand, dirt, and pebbles are sucked up by the dredge and washed over a sluice. This is a broad metal tray with large riffles across the bottom. The basic theory, as it was in the days of old, is that the heavier gold particles will be trapped behind the riffles as the water rushes over them.

Modern miners dredge a "promising" section of a stream and then remove the contents of the sluice for further refining. This may include small granite pebbles, old bullets or buck shot, iron, and gold. They say if you have found old bullets and buckshot, you're probably looking in the right place. The con-

As in the days of the Forty Niners, the gold pan remains the basic tool of the prospector.

A sluice box is used to separate the heavier, gold-bearing sands from larger rocks and river silt.

tents of the sluice are carefully placed in a plastic bucket. Each stone is removed and carefully washed during this process. Once the sluice box is clear, the miner sits comfortably on the bank and "pans-out" the contents of the bucket.

MINING FOR PLACER GOLD

For the purposes of our examination, the only real preparation is the purchase of a good quality gold pan, preferably one designed with riffles. They can be found at hardware supply stores in the Mother Lode for about $10. And even if you never use them again, they make great potato chip bowls for parties. Since gold panning requires that you stand in the water, it is advisable to bring along a pair of rubber hip boots. Also, take a small shovel. I prefer the basic U.S. Army folding shovel. A garden trowel also serves well. Lastly, take along a small magnifying glass, as the particles of gold may be very small.

Selecting a good location is everything in this business. Of course, if you opt to take one of the guided tours, you will be assisted in this endeavor. Try to select a stream that flows at a gentle pace, where wading is possible. Gold is many times heavier than water and sand. It settles along the outside banks of a stream at a curve and may be found beneath rocks and in the silt behind large boulders.

Using a shovel or trowel, dig down and take a scoop of dirt just above bedrock for panning. Hold the pan with one hand just below the surface of the water with the riffles facing away from you. With your free hand, scrub the dirt from any of the larger rocks and pebbles. Once you are sure they have been thoroughly washed, you can toss them back into the stream from whence they came. Once the large rocks and pebbles are gone, swirl the pan gently in a circular motion, still holding it just below the surface so that the stream water can wash away any of the lighter dirt. Throughout this process, the gold—just as it would in the creek—settles to the bottom of your pan.

Don't be in a hurry! Find a shady place along the bank and relax during this process. The gold has taken hundreds of years to find its hiding place, so why should you expect it to pop out in one swirl of a pan. As you continue the panning process, you should be picking out any pebbles that remain, again being careful to remove any dirt or sand that is clinging to them. Tip the pan at a slight angle away from your body and continue swirling. When you are left with only fine black sand, lift the pan barely above the surface of the water. Continue swirling the sand over the riffles in the pan and watch for gold. Use a magnifying glass to further examine the black sand. Now, try using a small magnet to remove any of the iron that is mixed in so as to make your process easier.

Should you find color in the bottom of your pan, use a small cotton swab to remove it or the tip of your finger. The gold flake or dust can be placed in a small plastic bottle for storage.

WHERE TO GO PROSPECTING

Prospecting is much like fishing. Once you find a good spot, keep it a secret. Although you can go prospecting at just about any time during good weather, the best time is late Spring or early Summer when the rain and snow melt has washed deposits down into the rivers.

According to a 1971 study by the U.S. Geological Survey of

minerals occurring in the middle third of California (the Mother Lode), gold can be found everywhere in the foothills—the same range that the forty-niners poured through a century ago. The survey did not reveal how much exists—only that it's out there. But don't expect to find any 150-pound nuggets lying around. Modern-day placer miners consider themselves lucky if they find a few small flakes.

Much of the Sierra foothill country is open to prospectors. Gold panning is permitted on most lands governed by the U.S. Bureau of Land Management and the U.S. Forest Service. However, it is not permitted within any National Park boundaries. If you wish to pan on a creek running through private property, be sure to get permission from the owner before mining. This brings up an important word of caution: Serious miners stake claims on Federal lands and may not welcome outsiders. This doesn't totally stop another person from panning, simply ask permission. Few professional miners feel threatened by an amateur with a gold pan. Many prospectors lead lonely, isolated lives and if properly approached, they can be a wealth of information.

Should you decide to head-out on your own, away from organized gold mining tours, you might want to contact the local ranger station and advise them. This serves two purposes. Rangers like to know who is out in the back country should a problem develop; and, they can sometimes provide helpful information on placer mining operations within their respective jurisdictions.

A do-it-yourself mining trip takes technical know-how and careful preparation. As with any backpacking trek or even a long hike, you should not go alone. Be prepared both physically and mentally for rough camping in possibly changeable weather conditions.

GOLD TOURS

Fortunately, for most of us, there are locations where outfitters will guide individuals or groups on mining tours. These give you a real opportunity to relive the days of old. On most tours, the group meets at a central location, usually in one of the rustic towns of the west. From there, it's a short drive followed by a hike into the claim. The guides provide all of the equipment and training. They help in selecting the perfect place on the river, and then they just turn you loose.

On the longer trips, visitors live in actual mining camps. Tents are pitched on wooden foundations and sleeping accommodations are consistent with early Civil-War-style cots. At night, everyone huddles around a campfire and listens as the guides swap stories of large strikes and nuggets. Then as the last embers die out, it is off to hit the sack for an early start in the gold fields. In the morning, you may work a sluice box or guide the nozzle of a dredge as it scours beneath a boulder. Then again, you may just enjoy going off to your own secluded spot to pan-out the diggings.

Whatever your desire, a gold prospecting expedition can be the ideal adventure.

Gold mining outfitters charge between $12 and $38 per hour for a family tour. Most guarantee finding gold and as a side attraction to panning trips, many take guests through actual lode-mines. This in itself can be well worth the trip.

Here are a few tour operators in the California Mother Lode:

Gold Prospecting Expeditions: Located at 18172 Main Street, Jamestown, CA 95327; (209) 984-4162. This is one of the larger outfitters. They are known to provide well-equipped trips every day of the year except on Christmas. They will even make arrangements to airlift guests into prime backcountry areas. Their one-day trips are especially good for families or persons with limited time to spend. All you provide is an old pair of work clothes and a sack lunch; they do the rest. On this trip, their guides lead groups through to a wash at Jackass Gulch or up to the Stanislaus River. Both of these sections were heavily mined by the forty-niners of old, yet gold is still found with only the aid of a pan and a dose of patience.

Matelot Gulch Mining Co: Mailing address is Box 1000, Columbia, CA 95310; (209) 532-9693. During the heyday of the gold rush, the town of Columbia grew to a city of 30,000 and was destined to become the capital of the new State of California. This was the jewel of the West, and is still preserved today in its near-original condition.

In keeping with tradition, John Baker who owns the nearby Matelot Gulch mine has devised an original adventure to let visitors see how life might have been in "old" Columbia. This

GOLD! Once you've seen it, you'll never mistake it for anything else.

is one of the only producing hard-rock gold mines that is open to the public.

While in Columbia, you may want to make reservations at the City Hotel for an evening. This restored building boasts the suite of Ulysses S. Grant and other fine rooms maintained as they appeared in the mid-1800's. The hotel is operated for the State of California by students at the Columbia Community College. Their service in both the lodging and dining rooms is exceptional.

BUT IS IT GOLD?

On a bright, sunny day, in the sandy bed of a creek, you are sure to see something sparkling in the sand. Gold? Doubtful. More than likely, it's iron pyrite—"fool's gold". While in sunlight pyrite is bright and shiny. The first test for gold is to take it into the shade. Pyrite will change colors, gold will not. As a second test, use a fingernail and try to break the substance. Some pyrites are very brittle, breaking easily. Gold, a soft metal, will only dent. The final and conclusive test involves using muric acid (a little expensive for the first-timer, but worth a mention). Gold is a very stable element and will not react with the acid. The other minerals bubble and dissolve.

Raw gold found in placer mining has a distinct color of its own. It's not too shiny, more a bright yellow. The glittering finish we're familiar with is cosmetically applied by a jeweler's buffing wheel. Some raw gold does have a sparkle (especially that found in hard rock mining), but it is unique and hard to mistake. As they say, once you've seen it . . . you'll never mistake it for anything else.

6

CROSS-COUNTRY SKIING

Amid the breathless landscape and silent solitude, a single hare scampers from a clump of brush and disappears behind a sagging pine. A loud pop breaks the scene as a frozen mass of snow tumbles down through the branches of a distant tree. Then quiet returns, casting stillness over the forest. Above, fluffy white cirrus clouds splash across a bright blue alpine sky. The winter drama unfolding before you is broken only by the sound of your skis as they ply through the snow at a constant pace. This adventure leads to a vast winterscape that remains hidden to most travelers.

Many of the more popular resorts and parks take on entirely different faces in winter. While in Yosemite along the Bridal Veil Campground area, my wife and I selected the Ghost Forest Loop trail. In the summertime, this entire area requires reservations several weeks in advance, and even in the winter is a favorite spot for nordic or cross-country skiing. We started through a gentle meadow and into the rolling hills. When we felt a little tired we stepped off the trail into a clearing, and I stamped out a picnic table in the snow. Turning our skis over to make a bench, we sat and opened our pack. The prior evening, we had prepared fresh fruit, a spinach salad, french bread, and two plastic containers filled with juice. We had not been dining for more than 5 minutes when we were interrupted by the rustle of a bush behind us. At first it was intermittent, and I went on peeling the skin from my orange,

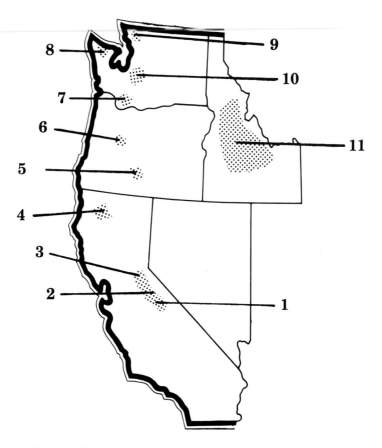

1. Yosemite/Badger Pass
2. Kirkwood Nordic
3. Royal Gorge
4. Castle Lake Nordic Center
5. Crater Lake
6. Mount Bachelor
7. Wilderness Freighters/Mount Adams
8. Olympic National Park—Tudor Inn/Port Angeles
9. North Cascades National Park—Mazama Country Inn
10. Mount Rainer Ski Touring
11. The Sawtooth National Recreation Area (Busterback Ranch; Galena Lodge Touring Center; Sun Valley Nordic Ski Touring Center)

The nordic adventure allows you to become part of the winter drama and witness another face of nature.

thinking all along it was only a clump of snow dropping through tree branches. But then it occurred again, much louder and as a strong, distinct shaking. My wife grabbed my arm and gestured behind my back. I turned slowly, only to come near nose-to-nose with a coyote. At first I was shocked and a little scared by the dog-like creature. We stared at each other for a moment and then I mustered up the courage to dig out my camera and snap a few frames. Fortunately, my model remained posed, studying us and probably wondering what the crazy humans were doing now.

Finally the coyote, apparently tired of us, scampered back into the bushes from whence it came. We finished our lunch, packed up our memories and returned to the trail. We skied another mile and crossed a small bluff. A meadow lay at the bottom of the brief downhill. My wife skied down the trail first and stopped part way across the clearing and signaled to me.

Directly in front of the tips of her skis was a set of fresh animal tracks in the snow. It was a rabbit moving across the frozen mass at a gentle pace. Judging from the small piles of powdery snow the animal had kicked, I figured that the tracks were only a few hours old at best.

We turned and followed alongside the tracks as they crossed the meadow. As we approached the stand of trees lining the valley, the tracks spread out. It was apparent that our rabbit had suddenly broken into a run. The trail cut sharply to the right, then doubled back, and cut another sharp turn. But why the sudden change of pace? Survival. There was another set of tracks, spread wide apart and running down a small hill directly toward our rabbit's tracks.

A few feet closer to the edge of the meadow, the tracks crisscrossed, but the rabbit was still very much in the lead. The pursuer's tracks were four-toed with distinct pads and short, pointed claws. The hind paw print was directly behind the front one and slightly smaller—clearly the impression of a hungry weasel. We followed the tracks around the perimeter of the meadow, then almost as quickly as they started, the rabbit's vanished under a hedge of small branches, and the weasel's stopped and then went off in another direction. On this day, the luck had been with the prey and the predator had to find dinner elsewhere. The luck had also been with us. A wilderness drama had unfolded itself for us during a simple one-day cross-country ski trek.

Observing wildlife is one of the many side benefits of nordic skiing. You will also find this sport has its relaxing and demanding moments, but most of all it is great fun for the entire family. School-age children up to middle-aged adults can pick up the techniques in an afternoon and get around comfortably on a tour. It is possible to pack younger children in a backpack carrier as long as they are suitably protected from the weather.

The remainder of this chapter examines nordic skiing adventures in the West. The trips described in this section are fairly easy for beginning and intermediate skiers. Guide services have been listed for those interested in alpine ski mountaineering.

SKIING STYLE

Nordic skiing has something for everyone. There are gentle tours across meadows and rolling hills; more advanced tours with steep downhill sections; and, finally, actual mountaineering treks on special cross-country skis. The growing acceptance of the sport by people who otherwise might not have availed themselves of winter recreational activities has led to the development of several resorts.

In most cases, our first thought when someone mentions skiing is of a person racing down a mountainside, his skis carving turns and spraying dry powder high into the air. Or a slalom racer cutting sharp turns while slapping the gates aside with his shoulder. Whatever the picture, the skiers are going down the hill. Gravity and their own body mass combine to produce most of the forward progress. Mass and gravity work *against* the nordic skier, on the other hand, even on a flat meadow.

This has led skiers and manufacturers of cross-country skis on a search for ways to make going up the hills easier. It was difficult finding a solution to the problem since skis travel down a slope whether they're pointing in that direction or not. Some of the earlier methods included preparing the base of the skis with pine tar and wax. This tried-and-true method is still used by most high-performance racers. There have been several new wax compounds, with special preparations designed for various types of snow and ambient conditions.

We all know that conditions sometimes change in the mountains, and it doesn't take an expert to guess that a change might require changing waxes. This led manufacturers to develop a variety of waxless skis. The first had narrow strips of mohair glued to the base. As the skier started up a grade and transferred his weight slightly forward, the fabric strips would cause sufficient friction to stop backsliding. Unfortunately, this development also resulted in slower, more laborious descents as forward progress was also inhibited.

The next generation of waxless ski had grooves or a "fish scale" pattern along the center third of the base. Applying the same principle as the ratchet in mechanics, skis could move forward with ease but were prevented from back-sliding. The

Taking a break to soak in the outdoors or enjoy a light snack away from crowded ski lodges is one of the advantages of nordic skiing.

only disadvantage of these waxless skis was that they tended to be slightly thicker and a little heavier. They make excellent touring skis for weekend recreation, but they are a bit too cumbersome for the racer.

Whether you use wax or waxless skis depends mainly on the type of skiing you plan to do. Fortunately, rental prices on equipment (skis, boots, and poles) remain about $9 to $12 per day. So you can easily try both techniques.

Here is a brief explanation of the various categories of trips you might want to consider.

Light Touring: These tours are similar to day-hikes and can include expert-level terrain or just a romp across a snow-covered meadow. The trails are usually well-marked and tracked. This is the most common type of skiing at the resorts in the Northwest. Some light touring trips can involve cutting tracks in fresh snow and may take you into the back country. These trips can last from 4 to 8 hours and many skiers pack a lunch in a small day-pack. This is the category where most beginners start.

Touring: This involves longer and often multiple-day treks through the back country. In some cases, trails are marked and machine-groomed but, in most cases, the only trail will be the track left by prior skiers if it hasn't snowed in a while. Skiers may pack extra clothes, camping gear, and food. This category includes snow camping and longer trips back to secluded lodges. Back-country experience and a knowledge of avalanche safety may be required before taking one of these treks. Skiing ability required can be either beginning, intermediate, or expert. Unlike most people who take up this sport, I first strapped on a pair of skis for such an adventure—a gentle seven mile trek across the back country to a lodge beside a frozen lake. We spent two glorious nights and I was hooked on ski touring.

Ski Mountaineering: This combines the best of cross-country skiing with climbing and alpine-style downhill skiing. As the name implies, it involves skiing into high alpine country where altitude and weather conditions can be very harsh. This can require great skiing and back-country ability. Anyone attempting one of these trips should seek a guide as well as education on winter survival and avalanche safety. Several of the mountaineering schools listed in the mountaineering chapter provide winter seminars and guide services for people who want to experience this type of alpine adventure.

Racing: Cross-country skiing offers a wide variety of racing opportunities for adventurers of every age group. Most of the resorts operate fun races on a weekly basis and include clinics to teach racing technique. In very basic terms, this sport can be thought of as running on skis. It is not just a question of endurance (although this is a major factor), but also technique and ability.

PREPARING FOR A NORDIC ADVENTURE

Planning a cross-country skiing adventure involves three basic requirements. Once you have selected the style of trip to take, you should consider where to go. Will the trip involve a cross-country ski resort? Or will you break virgin snow into new territory?

Many of the details have already been handled when you ski at a resort. Granted, you will usually have to pay a day-use trail fee ($5–$12). The trails will be tracked and groomed; loops will be identified by ability required (i.e., beginning, more difficult and most difficult); trail maps are supplied; the trails are usually patrolled; ski instruction is provided; warming huts and a day-lodge with food services are usually available.

On a back-country trip, you would need to plan for and provide some or all of these basic services. For instance, if you're using public lands, suggested trail maps can be obtained from a ranger station. Don't expect clear markings or nicely groomed paths. You will more than likely have to read the map and follow it throughout the trek. In this book we focus on light touring resorts. Guide services specializing in back country treks have been added for those who want more.

For light touring, I prefer the waxless skis. They are much less troublesome—all you have to do is pull them out of the rack, spray the base with silicon, strap 'em on and go—though they may not always be the best for the conditions of the day.

The choice of clothing you'll wear during and after skiing is crucial. Obviously, the primary concern is to keep warm. This can be accomplished by layering clothes and selecting outer garments that are water resistant. There are two complicating factors for the touring skier. You can think of them as the "ups" and "downs" of the sport. Cross-country skiing involves physical activity so your body perspires underneath the many layers of clothing. As you climb a hill, you may have the urge to shed garments; then as the slope turns downward, you may be surprised by the sudden cold. This effect poses a unique set of problems when coupled with the average climate in snow country. For these reasons, I usually dress in wool knickers with knee-high wool socks. I wear a turtle-neck shirt with a wool shirt over it, and a pair of knit gloves. While climbing a hill, I carry a heavy wool sweater and water-resistant wind breaker in my day-pack. I slip both of these on before starting a downhill run. For a hat, I wear a traditional herring-bone deer stalker, much in the tradition of Sherlock Holmes. If the

Advances in ski wear and equipment have made cross-country skiing available to the entire family. The key is to keep warm so everybody has fun.

weather is questionable, I exchange the hat for a knit wool ski-cap and wear a pair of powder-pants to keep my legs dry.

This combination of natural fiber garments and synthetic outer-wear keeps me toasty warm on the trail. As soon as I stop skiing for lunch or for whatever reason, I add another layer of clothes. Depending on the weather, this may include a pair of pants, a heavy parka, and a change of gloves. This is a necessary change no matter how warm I feel when coming off the trail. The principle is quite simple: once you stop skiing, your body is no longer generating as much heat and you run the risk of catching a chill.

Lastly, consider carrying a few convenience items in your pack. Some prefer a fanny-pack because it is carried on the hips and will not affect your center of gravity. But if a day-pack is small enough, this should not be a problem. Aside from the clothing mentioned above, your pack should contain water or other liquid refreshment, some light food snacks (trail mix for example), a compass, an emergency blanket (a "space blanket"), and a few emergency survival items (matches, knife, and small flashlight). If my light tour takes me into the back country, I supplement these with additional food, fire starter, and a small flare pistol.

If your trip is in the back country, make certain to leave word with a friend as to when you will be starting, your intended route, place of finish, and estimated time of completion. Tell the friend to notify authorities if you're late in returning. This is extremely important, as weather conditions can change rapidly in the mountains, and the chances of survival depend greatly on how soon someone starts looking for you. This procedure applies to all back-country travel including light tours of only a few hours duration.

There are several excellent books written on the subject of back-country skiing and snow camping. If you are considering one of these trips, it is strongly recommended you research and practice techniques. In this book we will be primarily highlighting resorts that offer skiers back-country scenery while providing groomed trails and either guided tours or patrols.

NORDIC TOURS

Yosemite—Badger Pass/California

This area boasts one of the largest back-country ski areas in the West. During the winter months, members of the Yosemite Mountaineering School operate the Yosemite Nordic Center. With 32 miles of set-track trails and over 90 miles of marked back-country trails, variety and beautiful winter scenery are the main themes of Yosemite in winter.

There are no trail use fees here. Morning and afternoon ski school sessions are available, along with day-care facilities for children 3–9 years of age. This is one of the best places to learn snow camping and avalanche safety. Five times each year, instructors lead trips along the unplowed Glacier Point Road to teach winter survival. For anyone interested in this type of travel, a seminar such as this is almost a necessity. Graduates

---

The grandeur of Yosemite in winter. A favorite one-day trip is over the unplowed road to Glacier Point and back.

can consider signing up for one of the many guided treks or even the annual Trans Sierra Trek.

Lodging is located in the Yosemite Valley. A skier's shuttle is provided between the lodge and Badger Pass Ski area. This is a very popular winter resort on weekends, so reservations should be made early. Contact the Yosemite Park and Curry Company for more information: (209) 372-1445.

Kirkwood Nordic/California

Voted the "cosiest" touring center in the West by *Cross-Country Skier* magazine, this center boasts the perfect combination of services, scenery, and trails.

Located near Kit Carson Pass along Highway 88, three interconnected trail systems wind through the dramatic valley. Kirkwood has long been a favorite of downhill skiers because of the Rocky-Mountain-like snow conditions. The valley floor is 7,800 feet above sea level and the surrounding mountain peaks top 10,000 feet. Because of the position of the ridges and the annual weather patterns, the snow tends to remain dry and powdery. The nordic trails offer diverse terrain and excellent skiing. Through open terrain and pine forest, over rolling hills and up steep pitches, the Kirkwood trail system climbs to 9,000 feet offering grand views of the High Sierra on a clear day.

Full ski school services are offered by the nordic center. This includes lessons from beginning to advanced, racing clinics, telemark, downhill, and guided tours by arrangement. Lodging is available through Kirkwood for one of six condominium complexes or several large cabins. Restaurants, night clubs, and a general store are also available at the resort.

For reservations and information, contact Kirkwood, P.O. Box 77, Kirkwood, CA 95646; (209) 258-7247.

Royal Gorge/California

Located off Interstate 80 at Soda Springs along the main route to Lake Tahoe and points eastward, Royal Gorge has been considered one of California's premier cross-country skiing meccas. In the best tradition of European resorts, overnight guests are treated to a lovely lodge complete with gourmet chef and hot tubs.

Nordic ski resorts have opened vast tracks of land in the back country. Their trails are well groomed and patrolled.

On warm, clear days, my family and I often spend the day at Royal Gorge. We ski out along one of the ridges above the Southern Pacific Railroad snow sheds. Near the edge of the cliff, we stamp out a picnic table in the snow and unpack our lunch. Before us, lies the peaceful vistas of Donner Pass and the main trans-Sierra freeway route.

Royal Gorge offers 300 km of groomed and double-tracked trails along with a full schedule of ski school programs for youth and adults. This is one of the best places to learn the sport. Take a morning class and then enjoy the trails in the afternoon. And for those who arrive in the evening planning to spend the night, Royal Gorge provides sleigh transportation into the lodge and hot mulled wine before turning in.

For more information, contact Royal Gorge, P.O. Box 178, Soda Springs, CA 95728; (916) 426-3871.

Castle Lake Nordic Center/California

This resort provides a great alternative to the major nordic resorts. It has 50 km of double-tracked groomed trails, a lodge, warming huts, fine food, and lovely scenery. But there is one distinct feature missing . . . the crowds! Castle Lake Nordic is one of the more popular in the Northern California, Southern Oregon area, but it is a fair distance from any of the major cities. When you travel to Castle Lake, you can almost be assured you won't have to play bumper-cars on the track.

This is a truly beautiful place. Situated along the western flank of a small valley, the resort is framed by major mountain peaks. While standing in one clearing, you can take in the views of Mount McGlaughlin, Castle Crags, Mount Shasta, and (on a really clear day) Mount Lassen. And, even better, the ambient weather conditions at this resort are ideally suited for nordic skiing because it is sheltered by the surrounding mountains and ridges.

To reach Castle Lake Nordic Center, take the main off-ramp from Interstate 5 for Mount Shasta City. Head east until you cross Lake Siskiyou Dam. Shortly after passing the lake, watch for a left turn onto Castle Lake Road. The main lodge is 6 miles further. Lodging is available with advanced reservations at the Castle Lake Chalet. There are several motels in nearby Mount Shasta City and in the town of Dunsmuir. One of my favorite motels is located at Railroad Junction in Dunsmuir, where the owners have refurbished several old railroad cabooses into comfortable suites.

For additional information, contact Castle Lake Nordic Center, P.O. Box 660, Mount Shasta, CA 96067; (24 hour snow conditions) (916) 926-5555.

Crater Lake/Oregon

If you thought this was a magnificent place in the summer months, come here in the winter time. The deep blue water of the lake appears even more like a blue gem when set against the white, snow-covered flanks of the caldera.

Though the visitor's center and lodge close after the first heavy snowfall, the lodge-like cafeteria and gift shop remain open throughout the winter, and the road from Klamath Falls is plowed up to the rim. Skiers can enjoy the great vistas and solitude by skiing portions of Rim Drive, the road which circles the caldera. Although it may be impractical to try to ski the entire loop (33 miles), portions of it make an ideal one-day light tour. You can end your trip at the cafeteria and enjoy a piping hot meal before your drive down.

Lodging is only available at the cities of Klamath Falls and Medford. Points north of the Park may not be accessible, as the roads are not plowed from the lake to the north entrance.

For additional information, contact Crater Lake National Park, P.O. Box 7, Crater Lake, OR 97604; (503) 594-2211.

Mount Bachelor/Oregon

This is another one of the more sophisticated resorts on the West Coast. Mount Bachelor Nordic Ski Area has had a long relationship with the U.S. Nordic Ski team and remains up on the latest styles and techniques of skiing. The center offers a variety of double-tracked, groomed trails leading from the main lodge area. The trails are noted for the variety of runs, from beginner's slopes to the most expert of downhills. Mt. Bachelor also offers a fully staffed ski school and hosts several special events each year.

Aside from this being one of the favorite nordic centers in Oregon, Mt. Bachelor also boasts one of the finer downhill ski resorts. It is an easy drive from either Salem or Portland, which is another reason to consider making lodging reservations early. The best bargain lodging and nearest towns are the cities of Bend and Sunriver. Shuttle services are available to the resort from both of these locations.

For more information about lodging and ski conditions, contact Mt. Bachelor Nordic Center, P.O. Box 1031, Bend, OR 97709; (503) 382-8334.

Wilderness Freighters/Mt. Adams/Washington

Mush! Mush! John and Lynn Simonson have developed one of the most unique nordic experiences south of Alaska. Their company, Wilderness Freighters, offers 2- to 4-day dog sled tours into the Mount Adams wilderness area. They have combined sled dog rides between isolated mountain cabins and some of the most dramatic cross-country skiing on groomed trails to bring their guests the finest of wilderness experiences.

This is the winter version of a fully-outfitted horse pack trip. The Simonson's guides take care of everything; from boiling the first pot of coffee to telling tales around a cozy fire place until the last embers die. And to provide a better experience, cross country ski instructors accompany each trip. The best features of a resort and a true back-country experience are combined in one.

A typical trip leaves from the Flying L Ranch, a Mount Adams country retreat worthy of a few extra days. Guests load into a snow cat that will escort the dog team as it works its way to the first cabin. Along the route, each guest trades places and enjoys a portion of the journey as a passenger in the dog sled. The team of seven Alaskan Malamutes makes quick work of the distance and by lunch you arrive at the first destination. A large tepee has been erected next to the cabin, and the staff are awaiting your arrival with a hot lunch ready. Then it's off to explore the back-country ski trails with one of the guides, or perhaps an afternoon ski lesson. The day ends with a real ranch-style barbeque.

The next morning starts early. The malamutes are hitched and ready and you're off to the next cabin to continue your adventure.

For additional information and a complete schedule of trips and rates, contact Wilderness Freighters, 2166 S.E. 142nd Ave., Portland, OR (503) 761-7428.

Olympic National Park—Tudor Inn/ Port Angeles/Washington

Throughout the winter season, nordic skiers are encouraged to experience the Olympic National Park at Hurricane Ridge. A concessionaire for the National Park Service has established an attractive resort with groomed trails, a single ski lift, day lodge, and ski school. But there is one other option when visiting the Olympics in winter—an option that mixes the charm of visiting an old-world bed-and-breakfast inn and a few glorious days skiing some of the less-traveled routes in the park.

Jerry and Jane Glass, owners of Tudor Inn in Port Angeles, Washington, have created just such a package. Guests at their inn can enjoy a day of guided cross-country skiing with the Glasses and their staff. Between the months of November and May, four park rangers from the Olympic National Park help the Glasses in guiding tours through this massive park. Depending on the weather, a typical trip might begin from Hurricane Ridge, or lead to the Olympic Hot Springs for a dip, or even a back-country excursion through the Deer Park Area. The Tudor Inn ski packages include lodging, breakfast, a packed trail lunch prepared by the Glasses, and optional ski instruction from one of the rangers.

This is a true winter escape for those wanting to experience the best of the Olympics in winter. It's a popular getaway for people living in metropolitan Seattle, so weekend reservations need to be made a few months in advance. For more details, contact Jerry and Jane Glass, Tudor Inn, 1108 S. Oak Ave., Port Angeles, WA 98362; (206) 452-3138.

North Cascades National Park—
Mazama Country Inn/Washington

This 10-room country inn is located in Northern Washington, in the heart of the Okanogan National Forest near North Cascades National Park. Fifty miles of groomed cross-country touring trails lead from the front door through the Upper Methow Valley. This lovely valley is framed by several tremendous mountain peaks and winds through large coniferous forest areas.

The Mazama Country Inn offers family accommodations, ski equipment rentals, certified instruction, and sleigh rides. The owners are glad to make arrangements for helicopters to airlift experienced skiers into the back country.

For more information, contact the Mazama Country Inn, P.O. Box 223, Mazama, WA 98833; (509) 996-2681.

Mount Rainier Ski Touring/Washington

Mount Rainier National Park has been a long-time preserve for cross-country skiers. The mountain rises to 14,410 feet and is the largest volcanic peak in the lower 48 states. This is one of the first places to get snow and one of the last to lose it, so their season is very long.

The ski center is located along the southern border of the park in Longmire, near the park headquarters. Here visitors can rent equipment, sign up for lessons, and obtain trail information. Lodging and special ski packages are available through National Park Inn.

For additional information, contact Mount Rainier Ski Touring, Star Route, Ashford, WA 98304; (206) 569-2283.

The Sawtooth National Recreation Area/Idaho

This state seems to have been discovered for the cross-country skier. There are several nordic centers and countless more back country trails through the several wilderness areas. There are enough of these centers to fill nearly an entire guide book. Along one major thoroughfare, I counted over a dozen. I have listed a sample of the resorts in the Sawtooth National Recreation Area, but be assured there are literally hundreds more in the state.

If you are considering a nordic adventure in Idaho, I strongly recommend you contact the State Travel Council for their current Ski and Winter Sports Directory. This booklet is invaluable when planning any type of winter trip in Idaho. It not only lists individual resorts, but entire ski packages. To obtain a copy, write to the Idaho Travel Council, Statehouse, Boise, ID 83720; or telephone toll free (800) 635-7820.

As an additional planning resource for this area, I have listed the various chambers of commerce and local tourism offices in the Appendix. These agencies have the most current information on resorts for specific areas of the state.

Busterback Ranch/Idaho

This is one of the true cross-country skier's retreats in the heart of one of the most stunning wilderness areas. The Sawtooth National Recreation Area boasts the largest unspoiled wilderness in the continental United States, excluding Alaska. And the 4500-acre Busterback Ranch is strategically located in the heart of the Sawtooth Valley. Accommodations are limited to 20 guests, but they provide day use for anyone who wants to enjoy the skiing. Their 24 miles of groomed and tracked trails wind through the entire valley.

To obtain more detailed information and current rates, contact Busterback Ranch Cross-Country Ski Lodge, Star Route, Ketchum, ID 83340; (208) 774-2217.

Galena Lodge Touring Center/Idaho

This complete touring center is along Highway 75, approximately 23 miles north of Ketchum, Idaho. Located along rolling and wooded hills, their 25 miles of groomed trails offer innumerable challenges and another perspective on the Sawtooth National Recreation Area. This is a complete cross-country resort, offering patrolled trails, lodging, instruction, meals, and ski shop. For more information, contact the Galena Lodge Touring Center, C/O Alpenrose, P.O. Box 1066, Sun Valley, ID 83353; (208) 726-4010.

Sun Valley Nordic Ski Touring Center/Idaho

Sun Valley has long been known for its world class downhill skiing. This cross-country resort carries that tradition into the nordic adventure. This resort provides 16 miles of groomed trails and contract guides for special back-country tours. They offer complete cross-country ski services, including lessons, rental equipment, night skiing, telemark lessons using the Dollar Mountain chair lift, and a complete ski shop.

For additional information, contact Sun Valley Nordic Ski Touring Center, P.O. Box 272, Sun Valley, ID 83353; (208) 622-4111.

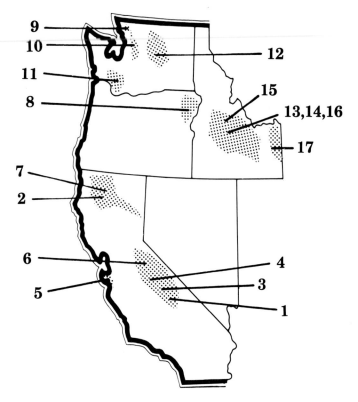

1. Lost Valley Pack Station
2. Marble Mt. Wilderness Packers and Guide Service
3. Cedar Grove Pack Station
4. Cherry Valley Pack Station
5. Sky Ridge Ranch
6. Mama's Llamas
7. Shasta Llamas
8. High Country Outfitters
9. North Cascades Outfitters
10. High Country Packers
11. Trail Blazer Llamas
12. Cascade Corrals
13. Sawtooth Wilderness Outfitters and Guides
14. Wildlife Outfitters
15. Rugg's Outfitting
16. Mystic Saddle Ranch
17. Teton Expeditions

7

PACK TRIPS
WESTERN STYLE

The words, "head 'em up, and move 'em out", conjure only one image for most of us raised on wild west films. This is the time when all climb onto their trusty steeds and gallop off into the setting sun. Over thousands of years, man has built a special relationship with his horse. It was often the sole means of transportation and, in the wilderness, might be the traveller's only companion.

This chapter takes us back to a time when freeways and jumbo jets were fantasy fiction. A time when life moved at a slower pace. There were concerns about water for farm animals, storing feed and supplies for the coming of winter, and worries of bandits stealing the mortgage money. This was the age of great exploration. Christopher "Kit" Carson had just opened a trail to the west and John Charles Fremont, another explorer, had just lost his bid to be the first President of the United States from the newly-formed Republican Party.

Trips over major mountain passes in those days were accomplished on horseback—Stanford, Hopkins, Crocker, and the others hadn't come to terms yet about plans for the new transcontinental railroad. Horses pulled wagons, they towed plows through open fields, and hauled mail from town to city. Ranchers found horses an invaluable tool. They were used on round-ups, and were especially sure-footed pursuing a stray calf. Cowboys could sit high enough to watch a herd's progress. They had quick access to lariat and weapon should the need arise. At the end of a long day in the saddle, the ranch hands would gather around a tall campfire and enjoy a hot meal dished out by "Cookie" who ran the chuck wagon. Then, after dinner, while Cookie and his helpers cleaned up, the bedrolls were spread around the fire, and one of the newer hands howled out a tune on his harmonica. As the last embers of the fire died out, the carpet of stars shone even brighter, casting their bluish light over the land. Everyone settled back and drifted off to sleep.

This scene was played out countless times over the last century and has never died from our imagination. We hold a fond place in our hearts for those great adventurers who trekked up the snow-covered passes of the Sierra Nevadas or Rocky Mountains in hope of opening new territory. Yet even today, this adventure trip into the high-country on horseback can be replayed. The rest of this chapter explores the options for travellers to experience the high country western style. This includes traditional western horse and mule trips and a new option—llama treks.

THE PACK TRIP AND OUTFITTER

There are several types of pack trips offered throughout the Northwest. These trips cover a spectrum of adventures from the "do-it-yourself" pack trip to the fully guided excursion. As with most sports, packers describe their services using a unique jargon. The first time I picked up a brochure from one of these outfitters, I was impressed at how inexpensive the trips were until I started to understand what some of the terms meant. Here are a few terms that will help when shopping for a pack outfitter:

Outfitted or *guided* pack trips. These rides span two or more days during which the outfitter provides everything except sleeping bags and personal gear. A guide will take care of setting up camp, cooking meals, leading trail rides, and cleaning up. These trips may be to one or more separate locations.

Continuous or *progressive* pack trips. Camp will be struck each morning and the group will move to another location. These can be either outfitted trips or "economy" trips, where

A guided trip through the Trinity Alps.

you provide all gear and food but the outfitter provides riding stock and guides.

Layover days. These are days where the camp remains in one place, and guests are offered the opportunity to take side hikes, rides, or just lounge around near the shore of a stream. Nothing shy of a day resting in the sun or bathing in a cool mountain lake takes the edge off the sore muscles. The number of layover days is what distinguishes beginner-level trips from the more advanced ones.

Spot trips. On these rides a guide takes you into a specific location and drops you off. On a specified date the guide returns to pack you out. People taking these trips must provide all camping gear and food supplies. They are a favorite of anglers seeking that hidden mountain lake where they can have it all to themselves.

Combination trips. These are usually guided rides that combine another type of adventure travel. Some outfitters offer to meet guests at the end of a whitewater rafting trip, while others might offer to meet seaplanes at mountain lakes for a few days of back-country fishing and then a return trail ride.

Dunnage or *hiking/traveling trips.* These are similar to a progressive trip, except the guide moves all of the gear and food from one campsite to the next while you hike along your own trail. This style trip is frequently selected by groups who want to trek without carrying a pack. The guides do not lead the trips but are only there to set up and move camp. You are expected to know enough about orienteering and hiking to make it to the next stop. When I was a Boy Scout, this was the type of trip we took each year.

Burro trips. At the pack station, you are loaned one beast of burden and bid farewell for the remainder of your journey. This is similar to the dunnage trip in the sense that an animal carries the gear; you get to do all the rest. This is a favorite for people who love hiking but don't want to carry along all the pots, pans, tents and other stuff.

Moonlight rides. For people who love to see lots of wildlife, this is a must. Some outfitters conduct these side rides on layover days when there is sure to be a full moon. You depart the base camp after dinner and return near midnight. As any park ranger will tell you, this is the prime time to observe wild animals as they are usually very active collecting food.

All of these trips require some degree of stamina and physical exertion by participants. As most of these rides are

Most pack trips head for the high country where hiking is difficult and trails hard to locate without a guide.

through high elevations or over mountain passes, you will have yet another factor to contend with. In preparation, spend time walking for more than a mile every other day for a few weeks. Try to include a city or county park and take in a few hills to allow you to get used to walking on uneven trails. Plan on doing aerobic work-outs in addition to the walks for at least 20 minutes each day, working up to the trip.

For the high altitude, plan on spending a few acclimation days at or near the trip's elevation prior to setting out. I found this an excellent excuse to hang out at the big Lake Tahoe resorts for 3 days prior to a ride. Not only was it fun at the lake, but the ride seemed that much easier—I wasn't winded at each bend while walking the horse.

Any person planning to take one of these adventures should be in good health. If you suffer from high blood pressure or cardiopulmonary ailments, consult your physician first. Also, if you have any special medical requirements or are taking any medication, let the outfitter know at the time you book the trip. I met a lady on one trip who suffered from a variety of serious allergies. The guides were fully briefed on what to do should she become afflicted.

Generally, plan on wearing a pair of smooth-soled boots on any of the riding trips. This could be a pair of the classic cowboy boots. The pointed toe and leather sole slips easily into the stirrups. A comfortable change of shoes can be carried in the saddle bags. Also, long underwear beneath a pair of blue denim jeans helps prevent painful chafing and keeps your legs warm should you encounter cool weather. Lastly, you should wear a wide brimmed hat and keep an ample coating of sun screen on exposed skin. The thin mountain air and high altitude combined can result in nasty burns that will spoil even the best adventure. On a llama trek, be prepared with a good pair of hiking boots.

When planning a guided trip, be sure to ask the outfitter for a list of what you should bring. I always ask the guide if there is any special comfort item he would take if he were booking the trip.

LLAMA OR HORSE

The appearance of llamas in the mountains of the Northwest has added a new dimension to outdoor adventure. These animals have a minimal effect on the environment and have led the U.S. Forest Service to open up lands that were previously closed to packers.

These mild mannered animals are sure-footed on steep craggy trails and completely adapted to working in high altitude. They are the principal beast of burden of the Indians from Peru to Chile. The ancient Incas are said to have used llamas to transport goods and supplies from sea level up to 16,000 feet in the Andes.

One of the most remarkable features of these animals is the minimal effect they have on the forest environment. In the forest, native grazing animals such as deer have associated predators like the mountain lion. The predator reduces the population size and thus the potential adverse effects of deer overgrazing. Domesticated stock, such as horses, sheep, or cat-

Llamas offer an alternative to the traditional pack trip. These sure-footed creatures are gentle on the environment and allowed in many areas closed to horses.

tle, will also overgraze an area if not properly managed. Over-grazing can result in the permanent destruction of plants and loss of soil from erosion. But, the llama requires only a small quantity of food compared to other pack stock. Typically, an adult llama will eat a 90-pound bale of alfalfa hay over a ten day period. This is much less than a horse consumes. As pack animals, llamas are capable of carrying over 100 pounds of equipment and supplies in special harnesses. Each guest on one of these trips leads a llama by a rope. The animals have been specially trained for their function and, because of their high intelligence and gentle demeanor, are very easy to lead.

Llama trips are run much like guided burro trips. Each guest must be prepared to walk and lead an animal. These adventures follow the great tradition of mountain treks through Nepal or Peru. The outfitters set up camp, cook meals, clean dishes, and take care of the stock (of course, guests can help in any of these tasks). Many tours offer layover days and special high-country fishing expeditions.

PACK TRIPS IN THE NORTHWEST

In this section, I have listed specific outfitters who offer various types of pack trips. This is only a sample. There are many outfitters in the Northwest. I would strongly advise you to contact the local chamber of commerce in the area you plan to visit (see Appendix for a complete list).

As with any guide service you plan to use, you should ask a few specific questions in advance. Begin by asking what their guides are like and how they select them. What do they look for when hiring a guide? How extensive a training program do they require for their guides? Ask about the service insurance coverage, their business goals, and past safety record. Determine exactly what services will be offered for the cost. Also ask if the outfitter can accommodate special needs such as extra layover days, special diet, programs for youth, and any other such personal concerns you may have. After asking the basic questions, if you still feel somewhat uncertain, request references. Make a few phone calls to people who have been on trips with this outfitter.

Once you have interviewed a few outfitters, you should be ready to book your high-country adventure. Remember to add a few days to the beginning of the trip to help acclimatize yourself to the altitude. If you are traveling to an area that you are unfamiliar with, call the outfitter and explain your needs. Often they may have cabins at the base ranch or know of inns in the vicinity. If not, call the local chamber of commerce and solicit their assistance in finding appropriate lodging.

California

Lost Valley Pack Station. Fred Ross, Blayney Meadows, P.O. Box 288, Lakeshore, CA 93634; (408) 238-0632. Offers burro trips, spot packing, and special guided trips by arrangement along the Muir Trail and Kings Canyon National Park.

Marble Mt. Wilderness Packers and Guide Service. 14446 N. Highway 3, Fort Jones, CA 96032; (916) 468-5401. Provides full services in the Marble Mountain wilderness of Northern California.

Cedar Grove Pack Station. Kings Canyon National Park, Cedar Grove, CA 93633; (209) 565-3464. This outfitter provides day rides, spot trips, continuous trips, and fully outfitted trips in the Sequoia National Forest, Sequoia National Park, and Kings Canyon National Park.

Cherry Valley Pack Station. P.O. Box 5500, Sonora, CA 95370; Summer phone—call Cherry Valley No. 2 through operator. They offer dunnage packing, burro trips, day rides, spot trips, and fully outfitted continuous trips in the Stanislaus National Forest. For the beginner or business traveler on a tight schedule, they offer a special weekend trip to a lake in the Yosemite Wilderness.

Sky Ridge Ranch. Box 9, La Honda, CA 94020; (415) 948-8398. Between May and October, this ranch nestled in the Santa Cruz Mountains is open to guests. From the trailhead near the San Francisco Bay Area, guests are guided along narrow trails to this modern wilderness resort where gourmet meals, hot tubs, tennis courts, and a variety of outdoor recreation awaits.

Mama's Llamas. Box 655, El Dorado, CA 95623; (916) 622-2566. Throughout the summer season, this outfitter offers fully guided llama treks through Point Reyes, Rubicon River, Desolation Valley, White Mountains, Kit Carson Pass, and the

Yosemite Hoover Wilderness. Once each year, they lead special treks in the Andes of Peru and Chugach Mountain in Alaska.

Shasta Llamas. Steven Biggs, P.O. Box 1137, Mt. Shasta, CA 96067; (916) 926-3959. Mr. Biggs is one of the foremost experts on llama treks. A former sociology professor, he was instrumental in designing packs and saddlery for these docile creatures. Three-, 4-, and 5-day treks are led through the Shasta-Trinity National Forest, Marble Mountains, and Klamath National Forest.

Oregon

High Country Outfitters. P.O. Box 26, Joseph, OR 97846; (503) 432-9171. This outfitter provides spot trips, progressive trips, and day rides through the Eagle Cap and Snake River Wilderness. Their specialty is family trips, and they offer a special whitewater rafting combo that includes a progressive pack trip and rafting through Hell's Canyon.

Washington

North Cascades Outfitters. Marianne Lesage, P.O. Box 397, Brewster, WA 98812; (509) 689-2813. This guide service offers spot trips, fully outfitted and "economy" pack trips in the Pasayten Wilderness Area. One of their best trips is up to Corral Lake. This requires a minimum of 5 days, but is well worth the effort.

High Country Packers. Bob Folkmen, P.O. Box 108, Issaquah, WA 98027; (206) 392-0111. Mr. Folkmen's company enjoys hosting families, groups and corporate teams for 1- to 10-day trips. They offer guided day trips and fully outfitted deluxe pack trips. This is one of the perfect escapes for travelers to Seattle. The ranch and trail head is only a short drive (about 2 hours) from the city.

Trail Blazer Llamas. Don and Kathy Johnson, 7819 NE 154th Street, Vancouver, WA 98662; (206) 573-1159. The Johnsons lead their llama treks throughout the wilderness areas of southwest Washington. Destinations include: Mount Adams Wilderness, Indian Heaven Wilderness, Dog Mountain, Lewis River Trail southeast of Mount Saint Helens, Goat Rocks Wilderness, William O. Douglass Wilderness, Glacier View Wilderness, Tatoosho Wilderness along the south side of Mount Rainier.

Cascade Corrals. The Ray Courtney Family, Box 36, Stehekin, WA 98852; (509) 682-4677. The Courtney family offers a full range of outfitted pack trips through the Glacier Peak Wilderness Area and Lake Chelan National Recreation Area. One of their special adventures begins with a seaplane ride from Seattle's Lake Union to the ranch. From there, you leave on a progressive pack trip to the Stehekin River, where you will raft through exciting whitewater and then pack back to the ranch.

Idaho

Sawtooth Wilderness Outfitters and Guides. Leo Jarvis, (summer) Grandjean, ID or (winter) Nampa, ID 83651; (208) 466-8323. This outfitter offers fully guided trail rides for an hour, a day, or a week. They specialize in fishing, hunting, and photo trips through the Sawtooth Mountains.

Wildlife Outfitters. 992 Pleasant View Drive, Dept. 10, Victor, MT 59875; (406) 642-3262. Through the months of June, July, and August, this outfitter has fully guided wilderness pack trips into the Selway Bitterroot Wilderness of Idaho.

Rugg's Outfitting. Ray Rugg, Saint Ignatius, MT 59865; (406) 745-4160. Mr. Rugg leads fully guided trips through the Bitterroot Wilderness. His goal is to provide a true wilderness experience for the people who decide to adventure with him. To accomplish this, Mr. Rugg manages each trip himself and, therefore, can only accommodate one group at a time. Bookings should be made in advance, with a little flexibility as to date in case another trip is already reserved.

Mystic Saddle Ranch. Jack and Deb Bitton, Redfish Lake Corrals, Stanley, ID 83340; (208) 774-3591 or 774-3311. This outfitter leads guided trail rides for an hour or a day, and fully guided pack trips for longer periods. Their trips include stops along the shores of alpine lakes and gentle trail rides through the Sawtooth Wilderness area.

Teton Expeditions, Inc. P.O. Box 218, Rigby, ID 83442; (208) 745-6476 or 523-4981. This family run outfitter offers memorable trips through the Teton Range of the Rockies. Their 4- and 5-day trips are fully guided. This company is also one of the major whitewater rafting outfitters and offers several combination horse pack/rafting tours.

8

"WHITE WATER THRILLS AND SPILLS"

It is 8 A.M. and the air is still cool, though the rising sun and clear blue skies suggest that the coolness will not last. Peaceful contentment abounds in the campground. The smell of fresh eggs and bacon sizzling in frypans is everywhere. And the only background noise is that of rushing water in the nearby river. For some reason, it seems a little louder, a little wilder than the night before when you set up camp. The water level must be higher. Or, more likely, the sensation comes from anticipation of the day's coming events.

As the breakfast dishes are cleared, a small group of people moves toward a tall oak tree where a man stands holding a clipboard. Within minutes, the group totals 18 men and women ranging from the ages of 8 to 68. A few are housewives, one works in a factory; there is a lawyer, a doctor, two nurses, a retired banker and his wife, and a police officer. Though they are strangers to one another, in an hour's time their differences will be forgotten and a lasting friendship will form. Inside, they already share a common passion: the challenge of the river.

The trip begins with a short bus ride to the put-in where the rafts are ready and waiting. On this adventure down the upper half of the South Fork of the American River, the bus stops at Chili Bar, a river-rat's outpost chiseled into a hillside a few miles northeast of Placerville, California. It's a colorful place where you'd expect to find rugged gold miners, pack mules, or the likes of Indiana Jones. The guides for the day explain the

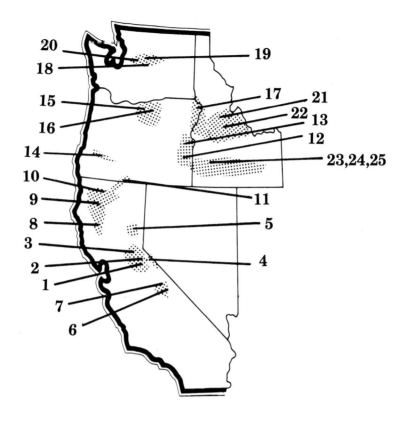

1. South Fork, American River
2. Middle Fork, American River
3. North Fork, American River
4. East Fork, Carson River
5. North Fork, Yuba River
6. Merced River
7. Tuolumne River
8. Middle Eel River
9. California Salmon River
10. Lower and Middle Klamath Rivers
11. Upper Klamath—Hell's Corner Gorge
12. Lower Owyhee River
13. Upper Owyhee
14. Rogue River
15. Deschutes River
16. John Day River
17. Snake River—Hell's Canyon
18. Wenatchee River
19. Methow River
20. Skykomish River
21. Main Salmon River
22. Middle Fork of Salmon River
23. Bruneau River
24. East Fork of Owyhee River
25. Lochsa River

safety rules and offer tips on paddling a raft through big water. Then, after being fitted with life vests and smoothing on a dose of suntan lotion, it's: "to oars!" The first rapid is only a short paddle from Chili Bar. It is a frothing row of waves and crossing currents that has been aptly named "meat grinder."

Whitewater rafting is an adventure for everyone. There are even rivers suitable for Great Aunt Mathilda. Fortunately, rafting can be as tame as a float trip down a gentle creek—or as wild as shooting the rapids of the Salmon, or the Zambezi River of Africa. Visitors to the Northwest are fortunate to have a large number of rivers to choose from that offer a range of rafting opportunities. Most river outfitters have no age limits, and only one requirement: that guests must be able to swim.

This is also the perfect adventure for the business traveler to any of the major cities in the Northwest. The various visitor and convention bureaus can arrange with outfitters for transportation to and from nearby rivers.

Many of the rivers are dam-controlled for hydro-electric power stations. This provides a generally constant flow of water throughout the summer season, and has, in fact, extended the rafting season. In the past and in many other portions of the United States, uncontrolled rivers run high during the spring thaw, offering large waves and lots of excitement. But then, as the dry weather continues, the level drops off and rafting becomes uneventful.

A controlled river works in reverse. The water levels do run higher during the spring thaw, but as the season continues and the days get hotter, the level increases. Power companies require more electricity on hot days due to increased demand; therefore, the dams release more water so as to generate more electricity. The net result is more exciting rapids.

SELECTING A RIVER

Although whitewater rafting is an adventure suitable for almost everyone, some rivers run tame while others require great skill to negotiate. For this reason, a classification system has been designed to help in selecting the right trip. Each rapid along a river is classified by degree of difficulty or, in

A typical class III rapid.

this case, raftability. The entire river run also receives a classification which is an average of all the classified rapids it contains. Along with cost and trip availability, the rating system is an important planning tool. These classifications apply to all rivers in the United States with the exception of the Colorado River.

Generally, there are two factors that affect a rating: gradient—the number of feet a river drops per mile; and the volume of water involved. As flow increases, larger waves may be generated when the water passes over boulders. Increased flows can also present some unique conditions in that rocks and timber may actually be forced down the river. This is important in uncontrolled rivers as the shape and placement of rapids may actually change depending on the force of the water.

While rafting on a class IV river, our guide prepared us for a large class V rated rapid around the next bend. There would be only one way for the boat to pass by the almost 6-foot-tall wave. And should we not hit it perfectly, we would all be swimming. Not a very pleasant thought at the time. We relaxed, resting our paddles in our laps, and let the raft drift on the swift-moving current; but as we approached the sharp bend, one thing became distinctly apparent. A class V rapid ordinarily sounds as though you are standing next to Niagara Falls. While you are in the rapid, all you can hear is the thunderous crashing of the water. But something was missing here—the sound. "Forward!" the guide shouted as we started around the bend. Each of us dug into the moving water with our paddles as we forced the boat to travel faster and faster. All concentration was in keeping up the paddling pace. We had to hit this one with enough speed to force the bow of the raft over the first large wave. If we didn't, the boat might stall and flip over.

The bushes and trees cleared from our view. There was no hole, no great raft-eating wave—just a few tiny bumps (known as "haystacks" because of the way the water curls up). We didn't even get wet. Apparently, the winter runoff was especially strong and the flow of water over the steep gradient had finally moved the large boulder aside and the rapid vanished. This is an example of how increased water flow can alter the rafting experience by taking away a wave. It can also move a boulder or log *into* the stream and create a large rapid where one never existed before. When contemplating a rafting trip, it is important to find out what the river's current classification is. Conditions may change dramatically on uncontrolled rivers.

The following is a description of the classification system currently in use:

Class I (very easy). This could be described as a moving lake with no noticeable rapids or waves. These stretches of river are perfect for flat water entertainment. Usually there is only a light current that can easily be paddled against in a rubber inner-tube.

Class II (easy). This is best described as a moving lake with a current and a wind blowing over the surface, causing small ripples. Once again this is a float-type of river, except that unlike class I, the water is moving much faster. Life vests must be worn and adequate precautions taken for swimmers.

Class III (medium). The river has a strong current, with 3-foot-high waves and equally deep holes. This is usually the beginning class for most of the commercially run rivers in the region.

Class IV (difficult). This requires more technical ability in the guide and crew. In order to pass through the rapid, the boat may have to be maneuvered around obstacles and through 4- to 5-foot waves and holes.

Class V (most difficult). These rivers are for experts only. The entire crew must be familiar with paddling techniques and whitewater swimming. Most outfitters require individuals to present a list of rivers they have rafted over the last year before admitting them on this type of trip. The rapids have only one route available, with large holes and 6- to 7-foot waves.

Class VI. Niagara Falls. Impassable. When encountering this class, rafts are beached and their crews walk around the waterfall to the other side.

SELECTING AN OUTFITTER

Choosing the right outfitter can be the difference between an enjoyable trip and a disaster. It's a matter of safety.

How do you find the best company? Begin a few months before the desired trip date. Read the outfitters' advertising literature. Does it give the impression that they are responsible and safety conscious? Next, call the outfitter. Find out how long they've been doing business. What is the size of the company? Ask what their guides are like, and what their company goals are. What type of training must their guides have before leading a trip? Does the outfitter provide this training or is past experience enough? How many rivers do they run? Outfitters should offer their clients a wide variety of trips to different rivers. Finally, what is the price and what about deposits, cancellation fees, and group rates? But before settling on the cheapest trip, think about where your money is going. A good outfitter pays insurance premiums, license and equipment fees, and workman's compensation insurance just like any other business.

RIVERS OF THE WEST

The Northwest is blessed with a variety of raftable rivers. There's something for everyone. And what's better, many rivers are close to major cities and make an excellent weekend or day-trip.

South Fork of the American River/California (class III)

The upper and lower sections of this river are usually run on separate one-day trips. This is one of the most popular rivers in central California. It combines fast-paced rapids and gentle stretches for floating.

Middle Fork of the American River/California (class III with some class IV rapids)

This is one of the more scenic rivers on which only select outfitters are permitted to run. At one point, rafters pass through a 90-foot-long solid rock tunnel.

North Fork of the American River/California (class V)

With fast-moving currents and BIG rapids through a steep-walled canyon, this river is full of surprises. The first 4.5 miles are filled with excitement but the end is not to be outdone, as rafts shoot down an 8-foot waterfall.

East Fork of the Carson River/California (class III)

This river carves its course for 21 miles along the eastern slopes of the Sierra Nevada Mountains. It combines fantastic views of the mountains, side hikes, a hot spring, and exciting rapids.

North Fork of the Yuba River/California (class IV)

Very few companies are allowed to run this river. The water is crystal clear and characterized by many excellent rapids. A road parallels the river for a long distance, so friends who may not want to ride the waves can catch the excitement on film. This is an excellent river to move up to after experiencing class III.

Merced River/California (class IV)

A fast and furious river that flows from Yosemite Falls. In comparison to many, this river has a mild gradient of only 45-feet-per-mile, but because of its granite base, the current moves very fast. Net result: big waves.

Tuolumne River (class V)

Fans of the film, *Indiana Jones and the Temple of Doom,* should recognize this as the river used for the rafting scene. Located near Yosemite National Park, the river flows down a grade of 40-feet-per-mile with many of the same conditions that exist for the Merced River. Reserve space early for this one. There are strong controls on the number of rafts permitted on this river and only a few outfitters have permits.

Middle Eel River/California (class III)

Only a few hours north of San Francisco, this river cuts its course through the Coastal Range mountains. The thrills take time to form on this one. The beginning is more class II, and gives everyone a chance to practice paddling before hitting the wet stuff.

California Salmon River (class V)

This highly technical river is one of the wildest rides in the state. Clear blue water rages down from the northern mountains and flows over large boulders. In many areas, there is only one way for the guides to shoot the whitewater. This river is limited to experienced rafters and, in most cases, full wet suits will have to be worn because of cold water temperatures.

Lower and Middle Klamath Rivers/California (class III)

Portions of these rivers are registered as National Wild and Scenic Rivers. From Happy Camp where the rafts are put in, the water flows between challenging rapids with plenty of time to soak up the sunshine and scenery.

Upper Klamath—Hell's Corner Gorge/California (class IV–V)

Eagles, osprey, geese, and great blue heron participate in this wilderness experience. The water is quick, the waves huge, and the birds fast if they're to catch dinner. Set in oak and fir woodlands, this river has only recently been opened to commercial rafting. Located near the mid-point between Portland and San Francisco, it provides travelers an excellent one- or two-day escape.

Lower Owyhee River/Oregon (class III)

Several have proclaimed this area the "Grand Canyon of the Northwest." After centuries, the Owyhee has carved its way through the great basin of southeastern Oregon. The scenery includes Indian petroglyphs, birds and mammals, and a few hot springs. As the water curves over the porous soil, haystack waves are formed. These guarantee excitement as rafts lurch over and around them, but there is also a fair amount of time spent floating in the calmer sections.

Upper Owyhee River/Oregon (class IV)

Basalt canyon walls close in on the upper portion of the Owyhee as the water flows faster through boulder gardens and steep drops. The echo of the rushing water blasts a cacophonous chorus as you slide downward.

Rogue River/Oregon (class IV)

Between canyon walls that average a few thousand feet high, the river lends new meaning to rafting. You remember scenes of a twig floating over the waves of a creek; only this time that twig carries passengers and has paddles. In one especially thrilling portion, rafts negotiate a succession of boulders and a fish ladder at Rainie Falls. Wildlife to be seen include deer, otter, beaver, and raccoon.

Deschutes River/Oregon (class IV)

Three- and 4-day expeditions are run down this river. Its close proximity to Portland makes this an excellent weekend escape. The river flows through the Warm Springs Indian Reservation and empties into the Columbia River along the Washington border. With a special character of its own, this river's rapids are large and boisterous, separated by gentle stretches.

John Day River/Oregon (class III)

This serene river runs through ancient fossil beds. Guides commonly point out geological formations and lead side trips to examine Indian petroglyphs. This is a favorite for people seeking a gentle, relaxing adventure.

Snake River—Hell's Canyon/Oregon (class V)

The Snake River winds through the southern half of Idaho from its origin in Wyoming until it reaches Hell's Canyon. Suddenly, the current picks up and water flows at 45,000 cu. ft. per second as it shoots through the gorge. At the deepest point, the walls of the canyon reach 6,600 feet above the river. This stretch has class IV and V rapids that are exciting to run but require experience. Campsites are set up near abandoned mines and cabins. This is one of the most spectacular trips in the United States. Shooting the waves of Hell's Canyon has been compared to the Zambezi of Africa.

Wenatchee River/Washington (class III)

One of the most popular stretches of whitewater, this river runs through the Wenatchee National Forest. There are several exciting rapids with names like Drunkard's Drop and Gorilla Falls. The river runs best during the spring and summer meltoff; its season is April 1 to August 1.

Shooting a class IV rapid on the "River of No Return."

Methow River/Washington (class IV)

This is an uncontrolled river that runs high during the spring thaw. The combination of high water volumes and steep gradients produces great rapids. There are several massive holes and equally large waves on this journey. The Methow is an excellent river for a second, more exciting experience after you've run a class III river.

Skykomish River/Washington (class IV)

Another of the uncontrolled rivers of the Northwest. This one combines boulder dodging along with a sharp gradient and high water. One of the more famous stretches is the rapid Boulder Drop where rafts slip through a waterfall-like shoot. The Skykomish is close to Seattle and perfect for a one-day adventure during its season (March 15 to August 15).

Main Salmon River/Idaho (class IV)

Known by many as the "river of no return," this formidable stretch of whitewater stopped Lewis and Clark on their expedition to the Pacific Ocean. As rafts progress, they are watched from shore by silent monuments of the past. Several abandoned gold mines and evidence of great Indian civilizations can be seen along the way. The river flows swiftly through North America's second deepest gorge. Several rapids add a thrill to the trip, but there is also ample time for peaceful floating and wildlife watching. The entire route is 96 miles long and takes 5–6 days to raft.

Middle Fork of the Salmon River/Idaho (class V)

When people talk of Idaho whitewater, this is the river that comes to mind. It is a solid class V run that starts out fast through some extremely difficult rapids. In the beginning, the primary effort is directed at rock dodging through the already fast moving water. After awhile, the gradient increases, and the ride becomes wild and flume-like. At one point, the river currents funnel into a trough and the boats are forced through a gigantic wave. This river is for experienced rafters who are looking for 5–6 days of pure excitement.

Bruneau River/Idaho (class III–IV)

This river flows through the high desert south of Boise and into the Snake River. Aside from presenting ample rapids, the river offers adventurers the opportunity to experience the desert environment. This is a less-traveled route and there is an abundance of wildlife to be found—from birds of prey to big horn sheep. Evening camp is set along sandy beach fronts where the guides prepare their special culinary feasts. Trips down this river average 4–5 days in duration.

East Fork of the Owyhee River/Idaho (class III)

This is the eastern relative of the Owyhee River in Oregon. Trips range 5–16 days in length, during which time travelers experience an ever-changing panorama of views and whitewater. No one environment typifies this wet route. At times the

"Spectators" along one of the many rivers in Idaho.

rafts enter steep canyons with walls extending 2000 feet above the water and, then around the next few bends, you "surface" among rolling hills covered in sage.

Lochsa River/Idaho (class IV–V)

Translated, the Indian name for this river means "Rough Water," and that is exactly what is there. Its clear water rumbles down steep flume-like channels at every turn, offering a variety of challenges to even the most seasoned rafting enthusiast. The season is short for this river (May through June) as it is not dam controlled and is dependent on the spring thaw. Trips average 2–3 days in duration.

RAFTING OUTFITTERS

Throughout the Northwest, there are outfitters offering excellent packages to each of these rivers. The list is so long, in fact, that it would be nearly a full-time job just keeping up with it.

Also, many guide services appear one day and are gone the next. Some are bought by competitors or just beaten out in this fast-moving market.

While researching this volume, I was given a list of outfitters by the Washington State Tourist Board. I began by sending letters to the people on the list, and was surprised when over half of the letters were returned by the post office. The rafting seasons on many rivers are short and are not the same from one river to the next. Moreover, a river you were able to raft on the prior year for 10 weeks may dry up in 3 this year. As you may be able to guess, this type of business environment may strongly affect cash flows and liquidity. It is survival of the fittest.

For these reasons, I have listed only a sample of the larger tour outfitters throughout the region. This is intended both as a service to the reader and a shopping list. You can start your search by calling these companies and interviewing their staffs, then contact the local tourism office or U.S. Forest Service for an up-to-date list and continue your search for the perfect trip.

All Outdoors Adventure Trips: 2151 San Miguel Drive, Walnut Creek, CA 94596; (415) 932-8993. This family business began by offering teen adventures in California and grew to offer adventures in California, Oregon, Arizona, Central America, Europe and Hawaii. They are a very safety-conscious outfitter whose first concern is that the clients have an enjoyable trip. Guides are selected for their personality and skills, and then must demonstrate their competence.

O.A.R.S. Sobek Expeditions: P.O. Box 67, Angels Camp, CA 95222; (209) 736-4677. One of the largest outfitters in the western U.S. OARS river expeditions cover Oregon, Idaho, California, Wyoming, Utah, and Africa.

Whitewater Voyages: P.O. Box 906, El Sobrante, CA 94803; (415) 222-5994. Another large outfitter dedicated to presenting clients the best of whitewater in Oregon, Idaho, California, Arizona, and Africa.

Turtle River Rafting Company: 507 McCloud Ave., Mt. Shasta, CA 96067; (916) 926-3223. Specializes in the rivers of

Northern California and Southern Oregon. They have also pioneered special interest trips, including kid trips, storyteller trips, and "Self-Discovery Through Challenge."

Lute Jerstad Adventures International: P.O. Box 19537, Portland, OR 97219; (503) 244-6075. This company boasts one of the more unusual adventure styles if you're so inclined. They call it, "Row it yourself." Lute Jerstad guides prepare clients to row rapids in specially designed two-person rafts. They operate on all of the major rivers in Oregon supplemented with trips to Idaho and various international ports of call.

North Cascades River Expeditions: P.O. Box 116, Arlington, WA 98223; (206) 435-9548. Conditions within the State of Washington provide exciting seasonal rafting on several rivers all year. This environment is unique and requires a special knowledge of the area in order to run successful trips. North Cascades River Expeditions runs trips year round. The selection of river depends on the time of year. Contact them for current conditions.

Downstream River Runners: 12112 N.E. 195th, Bothell, WA 98011; (206) 483-0335. Another established outfitter specializing in the rivers of Washington.

Salmon River Challenge: Salmon River Route, Riggins, ID 83549; (208) 628-3264. This outfitter specializes in one or more day trips along the rivers of Idaho. All trips are complete: cost includes camping gear, food, tents, and fun. They also offer trips in inflatable kayaks and dories, depending on their client's adventure style.

Teton Expeditions: P.O. Box 399, Riggins, ID 83549; (208) 628-3565. A family business that specializes in the unforgettable vacation in Idaho. In business for over 23 years, Teton Expeditions has found success in mixing whitewater rafting, trail rides, and fishing.

Canyons, Inc.: P.O. Box 823, McCall, ID 83638; (208) 634-4303. Susan and Les Bechdel specialize in rafting the Salmon River. They offer multiple-day trips down the "River of No Return" that can only be described as exceptional.

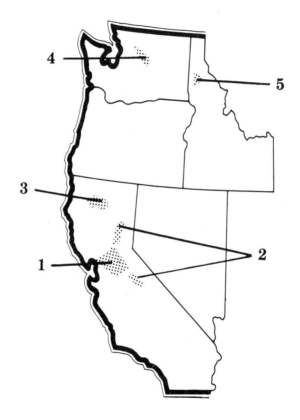

1. *Sacramento/San Joaquin River Delta*
2. *Lakes McClure, Don Pedro, and Oroville*
3. *Lake Shasta*
4. *Lake Chelan*
5. *Lake Coeur d'Alene*

9

HOUSE BOATING IN TOM SAWYER'S PARADISE

Imagine a sleepy place not too far away. A place warmed by the sun where two equally lazy rivers merge with the Pacific Ocean. The water flows at a steady pace, its currents lapping the shores of several inlets and sloughs that are covered with sagging willows. And under the eyes of a great blue heron, a swimmer dives into the water and swims toward a large rock. With little effort, the rock is scaled and the swimmer grabs a rope dangling from a tree limb overhead. She swings out over the water and lets go. There are loud cries of excitement from her friends as she swims back to her boat.

The boat is no typical craft. It is a boxy structure floating on twin pontoons and looks more like a large motorhome minus the wheels rather than a boat.

A BASE FOR OPERATIONS

These vessels are complete with everything for the well-equipped adventurer. They will in most cases sleep 6–10 people in comfortable bunks and beds. They have full bathroom facilities, kitchens, wet bars, stereos, and even propane barbecues on the stern deck. There is plenty of room to stretch out for a sun tan, and several places for you to dive over the side

for a quick dip in the water. Most boats are powered by a large outboard motor. This offers enough power for maneuvering and gentle cruising. But don't expect to pull a skier with one of these barges. Depending on the type of exploring you plan to undertake, you may find it advisable to tow along a ski boat or small fishing skiff. This way, the houseboat can be tied off at one location and shorter trips can be taken in the other craft.

The only confining factor is that you cannot leave the water. But this is by no means a problem. Throughout the region, the lakes and rivers offer such vast and diverse shorelines that there is no way to see all they have to offer in one vacation.

One of my favorite ways of using a houseboat is to live by natural time. I start by removing my wristwatch and making certain that none of the clocks on board are operating. I cruise across the lake until I find a small, secluded bay that strikes my fancy. When that perfect space for my first few evenings appears, I anchor just off shore, within swimming distance of land. And then I begin living my natural adventure—eating when I feel hungry, sleeping whenever I'm tired, swimming and sunning as the inclination takes me. I don't have to be at a given place at a specific time, and no one minds if I do nothing at all. Of course the friends and family that I'm with also begin living natural time.

It is amazing how quickly you can adapt to this life of little stress. As the sun sets and you first yawn, it is off to bed; and then, at the crack of dawn you rise to experience morning and another day. Breakfast sizzles on the stove while the sun warms the air outside. You dive into the water and are enveloped by its coolness, and then swim slowly back to the boat. The early morning hours are best for observing wildlife from the water. You are floating off-shore, the air is still and your scent is largely confined to the boat. It is quite common for deer and other animals to appear from the wooded shores and approach the water for a morning drink. Also, many raptorial birds become active just after sunrise. One of my first sightings of a bald eagle was from a houseboat.

But, best of all, is the almost total freedom enjoyed on a houseboat. After breakfast, should you feel like pushing onward, you just pull up anchor and slip down to the next inlet. Or, you might head into shore for a short walk; or plop under

Living by "natural time."

the spreading branches of a shade tree and dunk your fishing line into the water just as Huck Finn might have done.

BOATING SAFETY

From the moment you "sign on the dotted line" and agree to rent a houseboat, you should think safety. Most of the reputable resorts will have a staff person to give you a tour of the boat and explanation of its safety features. This may be the kind of tour where the guide points at a settee and says, "life jackets are under there," then knocks on a closet door by the aft deck and adds, "fire extinguisher's in here. Now let me show you the stereo system. . . ." This type of tour is fine as far as it goes, but you should not leave it at that. An accident always happens to the other guy, until you're distracted while frying on the stove and a grease fire flashes up.

Once the familiarization tour is over and before you begin loading all your gear on board, get the group together for a safety talk. Open one of the life jacket containers. This might be more difficult than you expect. Although the Coast Guard requires the preservers to be readily available, the container may not have been opened since before the last maintenance. On a boat I was recently on, this was evident from the several coats of varnish that had effectively sealed the container. My friend and I had to work for ten minutes with large screw drivers to pry it open.

Next, remove one of the vests and fit it on someone. Personal flotation devices come in a variety of sizes and shapes. Some are held by tie straps, while others have plastic clips and a waist strap. Show your guests by demonstration how to adjust one of these vests. They should fit snugly, and the front part of the bodice where the vest comes together should not lift up to obstruct the chin. At this time, if your passenger list includes any children under age 12, fit them with their life jackets. The law requires they wear one any time they are outside the houseboat's main cabin.

Once you've returned the life jackets to their container, move on to the fire extinguishers. Inspect each of these to insure they are charged. This can be accomplished by simply reading the gauge at the top of the unit. Show your guests how to remove an extinguisher and note the instructions for use printed on the side of the unit. This should include how to release the safety and how to attack a fire. In concluding the basic safety talk, remind your guests to stay clear of the fore-deck in front of the helm while the boat is in operation. Also, make sure everyone understands that diving into the water while the boat is moving could lead to major injury from propellers under the boat.

As the other guests begin loading food and personal gear on to the boat, take a moment with the primary crew members for the trip. Talk about specific boat operations: how to operate the motor, fueling procedures, turning on and off fresh water pumps and valves for the propane tanks. Regardless of the freedom offered by the sport of houseboating, there are some important boating guidelines that must be followed by the crew to insure a successful trip. These rules were enacted by Congress to prevent collisions and they apply to houseboaters. Yet some people choose to ignore them. While cruising across Lake Shasta in Northern California, I found myself relaxing on deck, watching a ski boat zip past me towing a single skier. They were skipping across the water, and the skier was cutting turns across the boat's wake sending up a fan-tail of water with each cut. The people on the tow boat must have been just as mesmerized by the skier's expertise as I was because they were suddenly on a collision course with a small aluminum row boat. The ski boat's driver spotted the small craft and swung a sharp left narrowly avoiding a crash, but the large wave that resulted from the maneuver swamped the small boat.

A copy of the current rules of the road should be obtained from the marina prior to departing on your adventure. Beyond these guidelines, you should be aware of some common sense boating safety practices. The helm is for all intents and purposes a part of the main dining room or kitchen area. This is usually the center of activity, and whoever is driving the boat must avoid distractions. Visibility is another limiting factor from inside one of these barges. I found it beneficial to set up a "watch" schedule among some of the younger passengers. Their duty was to help point out obstacles and other boats while we were underway. They would stand at the very tip of the bow with instructions to point at objects that were within our path or approaching us.

ON-THE-WATER

When planning a houseboating adventure, start by selecting where you would like to go. The next step is to contact marinas on the various lakes and rivers for estimates and availability of the vessels. While interviewing a representative from the marina, there are some questions that should be answered. How long have they been in business? What is their goal in business? On what schedule are their boats serviced? Do they do the service on-site or contract with another marina? How large is their fleet and what about sleeping space and floor plans? How old is their fleet? Do they supply fuel (both propane and gasoline)? What are the kitchens like? And, finally, what operating instruction do they include with rental?

Armed with these questions, you should be able to make an educated decision about which marina to select. As with any outfitter or guide service, don't be tempted to jump at the first low price. Operating a houseboat rental operation is expensive. Aside from maintenance and equipment costs, they must consider insurance, training, worker's compensation, facilities, and a good deal more.

Below, we outline first the various flat-water recreation sites throughout the region and then suggest a few marinas to start your search. Be aware that this list of operators is only a starting point. Contact the local Chamber of Commerce, Visitor and Convention Bureau, or State Tourism Office for a more complete list. A reference list of these organizations can be found in the Appendix of this text.

Sacramento/San Joaquin River Delta

More than any other location west of the Mississippi, this one best typifies the dream of two boys playing hooky to go fishing and the beginning of a great adventure. The hundreds of sloughs, inlets, and narrow passages are hemmed in by trees and shrubs, their sagging branches dangling into the slow-moving water. Piloting a boat away from one of the main channels, you immediately feel a sense of isolation and tranquility as you begin exploring.

Although thousands of people visit the deltas on a typical summer weekend, there are hundreds of miles of room for everyone. On one trip, we tied-off on the southern shore of Lost Isles (a modest marina near Stockton, California). Our experience was only interrupted by the occasional chirp of a bird, or the splash of water as we took a swim; yet we were only a short hike from civilization. Some of the more remote get-away spots for relaxing include Three Mile Slough, Steamboat Slough, Hogback Island, and Lost Isle. And for those days when the solitude becomes too much, there are several resort-like settings in the area: Discovery Bay, Bethel Island, Paradise Point, King Island.

Because of the miles of open waterways, it is important to plan your course and destination before actually moving the boat. This is not to say that you shouldn't make impulsive moves to alternate anchorages; but you do need to consider such factors as fuel and time. For this reason, it would be worthwhile to purchase a nautical chart of the area in question or even a special cruising guide. There are several books available to fill this need, but I prefer Hal Schell's *Guide to Cruising and Houseboating the Delta*. This publisher also produces a delta map that is sold in most of the marinas in the area. The chart provides not only navigation and water depth information but lists resorts and unique points of interest.

One of the special places noted in most of the books is the delta community of Locke. Situated along the banks of the Sacramento River, this town was entirely built and occupied by Chinese settlers to the area. There are several historic and restored buildings to see, including one of the town's old gambling halls that is now a museum. Boaters can pay a tie-up fee at Walnut Grove and make the short mile walk to town. Locke can also be reached by car.

There are several marinas advertising houseboat rentals in the delta region. Here is a sampling of a few of the larger operators. As with many of the other adventures described, I would recommend interviewing their representatives and making extensive comparisons before coming to a decision. This is by no means an inclusive listing. Contact the chambers of commerce for Sacramento or Stockton, or the appropriate visitor and convention bureaus, for additional listings.

Delta Country Houseboats, P.O. Box 246, Walnut Grove, CA; (916) 776-1741.

Herman and Helen's Houseboats, Venice Island Ferry, Stockton, CA; (209) 951-4634.

Holiday Flotels, Delta, 11530 W. 8 Mile Road, Stockton, CA; 95209; (209) 477-9544.

Paradise Point Marina, 8095 N. Rio Blanco Road, Stockton, CA 95209; (209) 952-1000.

Lake McClure, Lake Don Pedro, Lake Oroville/California

These manmade lakes lie among the rolling foothills of the California Mother Lode at the southern end of the region covered in this book. They typify the flat water recreation spots that stretch along the eastern border of the Sacramento and San Joaquin Valleys. They are easily accessible with plenty of camping sites and rental cabins; water levels drop a bit by the end of the summer, but this is not a major problem; their tree-lined shores are attractive; and, best of all, the air temperature is usually warm-to-hot in the summer. These factors add up to a perfect houseboating adventure.

These lakes offer another attraction for summertime anglers. They are well stocked with trout and bass, both fine-tasting treats when cooked on the grill. Many of the houseboating marinas provide special tips as to where the fish are biting, and a few even offer cooking tips for when you've caught the critters. For myself, the fishing is secondary. I drop my line into the water with its token worm firmly attached, lay back in a deck chair, tip my hat to block the sun, and soak up the solitude. And then, depending on my mood, I might fire-up the engine and cruise across the lake to explore another cove.

Most of these lakes will attract several local folks on the weekends, so you should plan to enjoy having a few neighbors on the water during these times. Weekdays, they are less crowded, and there is more room to stretch out and explore.

Here are a few of the marinas and resorts offering houseboat rentals on these lakes.

Lake McClure:
Barrett Cove Marina, Star Route, LaGrange, CA 95329; (209) 378-2441.

Lake Don Pedro:
Lake Don Pedro Marina, Star Route, Box 81, La Grange, CA 96051; (209) 852-2369.
Moccasin Point Marina, 11405 Jacksonville Road, Jamestown, CA 95327; (209) 989-2383.

Lake Oroville:
Lime Saddle Marina, P.O. Box 1088, Paradise, CA 95969; (916) 534-6950.

Lake Shasta/California

Three hundred-forty miles of shoreline surrounded by mountains and tall pine trees adorns one of the largest lakes in Northern California. If lakes were measured by total shoreline, Shasta would be near the top of the list. Four major tributaries keep the water levels high during the spring and summer thaw: Pit River, Squaw Creek, McCloud River, and Sacramento River. At the dam along the southern shore, the mighty Sacramento River begins winding through the valley, supplying water to fertile soils and eventually emptying into San Francisco Bay.

Houseboating on Lake Shasta is an adventure of ever-changing sights and diversions. There are many more shores than could easily be explored within the usual one- or two-week vacation. And this doesn't include the many side attractions. The lake is a focal point for sightseeing trips throughout the Shasta/Cascade region. There are caves to explore, tours of the dam itself, mountains to climb, several islands, and the best fishing you could ask for.

Houseboating on Lake Shasta.

Along with rental of the houseboat, many of the marinas will rent ski boats or the hottest attraction since the string bikini, jet skiis. These may add a little stress to the Master Card, but are well worth it for a day or so.

Lake Shasta is located along the I-5 freeway approximately 30 miles north of Redding. There are several marinas here offering houseboat rentals. I have listed a few of the larger companies. For a complete and current listing of all the marinas, contact the Shasta-Cascade Wonderland Association, Tourist Information Center, 1250 Parkview Ave., Redding, CA 96001.

Bridge Bay Resort and Marina, 10300 Bridge Bay Road, Redding, CA 96003-9418; (800) 752-9669.

Digger Bay Marina, P.O. Box 1516, Central Valley, CA 96019; (800) 752-9669 or (916) 275-1522.

Holiday Harbor, P.O. Box 112, O'Brien, CA 96070; (800) 258-BOAT or (916) 238-2383.

Silverthorn Resort, Inc., P.O. Box 4205, Redding, CA 96099; (800) 332-3044.

Lake Chelan/Washington

Winding its way through the Northern Cascade Range, Lake Chelan offers both wilderness and resort perspectives. Along the northwestern flanks, high mountains and dense forests wrap the lake in seclusion, while closer to the dam—where the water flows into the Columbia River—the lake is lined with several resorts. The more rolling hills here are dotted with golf courses, tennis courts, fine restaurants, and lodges.

The lake has become one of the favorite get-away spots for residents of Spokane and Seattle. Situated midway between the cities, it is easily accessible in a day's drive. And there is no better way to relax than in the comfort and seclusion of a houseboat. While the others pretend to enjoy the crowded resorts, standing in queues at the tennis centers, you find solace in being away from it all—just your friends and nature as you cruise off into the setting sun.

Houseboats can be rented from *Lake Chelan Houseboat Rental,* Route 1, Box 368, Manson, WA 98831; (509) 687-3928.

Lake Coeur d'Alene/Idaho

This 22-mile-long lake sits in one of the most spectacular wilderness areas of the lower 48 states. The shore is lined by thick coniferous forest that hosts an abundance of wildlife. On a clear sunny day, the stark contrast of the sparkling blue water against the earth and green woods is like no other view. One can easily see how this lake has become known as one of the loveliest in the Northwest.

The lake is located just off Interstate 90 after entering the panhandle of Idaho from Spokane, Washington. Its waters run in a near-straight course 22 miles long and 2 1/2 miles wide. There are several secluded coves, providing perfect anchorages for houseboats. As with many of the other smaller lakes in the area, the fishing here is excellent. Anglers not familiar with all of the seasonal "spots" should inquire at the marina for a few tips before heading out. And if the 110 miles of shoreline along the main lake is not a sufficient attraction, you can guide your boat up the shadowy Saint Jo River for an additional 30 miles. This river is the highest elevation navigable waterway in the United States. The river takes boaters through a fjord-like channel surrounded by thick forests. Each day during the summer months, three cruise ships with up to 400 passengers navigate the waters of the Saint Jo for a one day excursion.

Information on houseboat rentals on Lake Coeur d'Alene can be obtained through the *North Shore Marina of the Coeur d'Alene Resort and Conference Center.* Telephone: (208) 765-4000.

10

BARNSTORMING

"Just relax, now. Ready? Here we goooooo. . . ." Outside the open-air cockpit, the world rolled over. Suddenly the sky was where the earth should have been and, for a moment, my orientation was lost. Then we plunged downward, or was it upward. Well, anyway the earth jumped towards us, and the force of the fall tugged at my cheeks. It was as though I was plunging down a roller coaster, but this one accelerated faster. The altimeter seemed to be spinning downward. Then the engine roared, and the horizon appeared again before us. All I could do was scream my excitement; or so it seemed. I was probably screaming during the entire roll and dive, it was just now that I was hearing myself. The gauges on the small instrument panel were climbing once again as the pilot reached up from his open cockpit in the rear and tapped my shoulder. "Still with me? One more time?"

I was hooked. As hooked as the Wright Brothers must have been after the first flight at Kitty Hawk. I gave the thumbs up and thought the pilot gave a chuckle. We began climbing, the plane constantly rolling wing over wing. It was like nothing I had ever experienced before. As we reached 7,000 feet, we pulled back and made a complete loop. My weight transferred against the harness that held me in as we finished the maneuver.

As we leveled out again, I glanced to one side and studied a large billowy cloud that appeared like a tower next to us. I could now imagine how the earlier pilots must have felt during the First World War, and I wondered when the Red Baron's plane would appear.

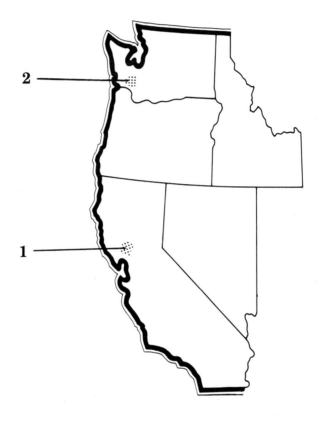

1. *Aero Schellville—Sonoma Valley*
2. *Frank Brickey Aviation—Mount Saint Helens*

There are several aviation adventures available to people who do not pilot their own planes. Generally speaking, there are two reasons we consider chartering an aircraft: basic transportation and excursion flights. The latter category includes stunt pilots that take their guests through aerobatic maneuvers and "bush" pilots who fly you over remote areas.

Many of us have visited an airshow at one time or another or, at least, watched the daring exhibitions on television. We have watched small biplanes climb straight up in the sky as though they were rockets, trailing a plume of white smoke in their wake. And then, just as suddenly, they stall and roll downward in a dive. Our hearts pause as we watch in horrifying fascination only to be thrilled as the craft levels off just above the airfield. At the conclusion of the show, when the plane taxis slowly across the field, we leave with a feeling of satisfaction and more stories to tell our offspring. Yet there is one question that gnaws at many of us as we think back on such dramatic shows: what was it truly like to be inside that plane?

Aero Schellville can make this dream a reality. Located in the beautiful Sonoma Valley, this company offers both gentle air tours and aerobatic flights over the California Wine Country. On their basic tour, a single passenger in the front seat of their biplane is taken over some of the most attractive areas of the Sonoma and Alexander Valleys. Just before returning to the field, the pilot rolls the plane into a single sharp barrel roll.

For those wanting to experience the absolute force of this World-War-I vintage craft, sign up for the full aerobatic treatment. As soon as you achieve altitude from take off, the pilot begins a routine of loops, spins, and rolls that mimic maneuvers of early fighter pilots. From the front seat—where the observer rides—you experience the total effect of the flight. And upon landing, you can think back upon your experience, knowing that few have ever done the same.

For more information, contact: *Aero Shellville,* 23982 Arnold Drive, Sonoma, CA 95476; (707) 938-2444.

Frank Brickey Aviation brings another attraction into the realm of specialty flights. Unlike the other barnstorming adventures, where the thrill is basically man and machine, these

The desolation around Mount Saint Helens. One of the best ways to get a closer look is from the air.

flights in Southern Washington take travelers to see one of nature's true wonders. On a brief excursion trip, guests are flown over the steaming and still-active Mount Saint Helens. As most readers will remember, this mountain erupted in 1980, sending a shower of ashes over most of the Northwest. From the air, you will be able to comprehend the magnitude of the forces that ripped the mountain's side open.

For more information about these tours, contact: *Frank Brickey Aviation,* 1109 E. 5th Street, Vancouver, WA 98661; (206) 699-5489. Reservations are a must for this one.

11

FLYING
ON WATER

The morning is young and fresh, alive with the sounds of day-break. You have just finished packing up your napsack. The large kitchen tent falls like a deflated balloon, and you watch as the guides fold the heavy canvas into a neat sack. Thoughts of the kitchen tent stir memories of last evening's meal, when the guide expertly filletted and battered the large trout caught only a few hours earlier. What a meal that was.

As the last items are stowed away, the sound of an airplane engine breaks the quiet above the pine trees. It draws nearer, and as you look out across the lake, a small seaplane glides downward and skips onto the surface of the water. Then the engine idles down and the plane drifts slowly towards the shore.

The plane comes to a stop at the small dock. As a few of the guides help load your gear into the storage hold of the plane, you have a moment to bid your hosts farewell. This has been one of the most restful weeks you can remember in a long time. Your work back home seems like a distant fantasy—an island of isolated memories surrounded by a tranquil sea. After making your final good-byes to this back country retreat, you board the craft.

The pilot, a brawny man who looks as though he could have swung an ax with Paul Bunyan, gives you a few brief instructions about fastening your seatbelt. You have one last chance to wave at your new friends, as the engine fires. Although this

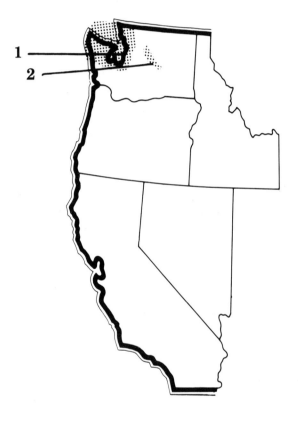

1. *Lake Union Air*
2. *Stehekin Air Service*

A seaplane prepares to depart on "nature's runway."

is the end of your trip, you are off on one final adventure. A seaplane adventure.

NATURE'S RUNWAY

The sight of airplanes with long pontoons landing on remote lakes of the Northwest became commonplace soon after the first seaplanes were designed. They provided sportsmen and land owners a unique method for accessing lands where no automobiles could reach. One of the truly attractive features was that you didn't have to clear the forest to lay an asphalt or gravel strip. You just set down on Mother Nature's own runway. Several portions of the Pacific Northwest remain inaccessible except by seaplane. That is, unless you have a horse or sturdy mule who can swim.

Seaplanes have opened a unique opportunity to anyone wanting to experience new sections of the back country on a limited time schedule. Many rafting outfitters along the rivers in Idaho and several horse packing outfitters offer bookings on seaplanes. Though many of their guests might find it preferable to travel by car to a meeting place and then spend an extra day or so reaching the outfitter, many more like the thought of quick access. And, as an added feature, flying for miles over huge timber stands only to drop down and land on water is a unique adventure in itself. Yet, of the people using seaplanes in the Northwest, those who travel to remote lakes are truly in the minority. One of the larger charter companies operates daily service from Lake Union in the heart of downtown Seattle to the San Juan Islands, Puget Sound, Victoria, and Vancouver, B.C. Their next most popular trip is a seaplane excursion over the metropolitan area. Finally, they make a few trips into the back country at the request of outfitters.

Seaplanes have been around for quite awhile. The very first Pan Am China Clipper was a scheduled seaplane. It took off from Treasure Island in the San Francisco Bay, and flew to Honolulu, Midway, Wake Island, Guam, Manila, and finally to its destination, Hong Kong. And, along with the Clipper, Howard Hughes' Spruce Goose was an amphibious craft—the largest of its time.

During their day, amphibious planes were designed to transport people and cargo to places not serviced by airports. Any sea port served the berthing function for these huge craft. Nowadays a plane can lift off from a few hundred feet of lake along Seattle's east side and land at the harbor entrance to Victoria. This cuts short the ride by ferry to one of the most beautiful cities in British Columbia.

These planes can also make connections with a houseboat resort on Lake Chelan or take you on into some of the remote portions of Idaho. One of the more common routes travels the length of Lake Chelan. Guests leave the southern city of Chelan and fly through the rugged peaks of the North Cascades National Park to reach Stehekin, at the northern tip of the lake. Not only is there a lovely lodge here, but this is also the starting point for pack trips and winter ski treks.

Seaplanes along Puget Sound provide support for more traditional means of transportation.

NORTHWESTERN SEAPLANE TRIPS

Trips aboard these float planes are considered true adventures of the Pacific Northwest. Only two things are required—lots of water and beautiful destinations. Neither of these is lacking. Schedules are fairly flexible; there's rarely a delay on the ground because of too much air traffic; and, most scheduled seaplane services can be cheaper than renting an automobile. They certainly provide faster service to the destination.

Here are a few of the prominent seaplane operators in the Northwest who provide year-round service.

Lake Union Air/Washington. One of the largest seaplane services. They offer scheduled daily flights from Seattle to Victoria Harbor, B.C.; San Juan Islands (Roche Harbor, Friday Harbor, Rosario Harbor, and Lopez), WA; Oak Harbor, WA; and Vancouver, B.C. Any one of their ten seaplanes is available for charter into the back country, and they will gladly meet passengers at downtown hotels in one of three vans. For those not wanting to travel too far, Lake Union Air offers special Seattle excursions by seaplane. This is a relatively inexpensive way to see the sights of the city and Puget Sound.

For schedules or more information, contact: Lake Union Air, 1100 Westlake Ave. N., Seattle, WA 98109; (206) 284-0300.

Stehekin Air Service. The town of Stehekin is located at the northern tip of Lake Chelan in the heart of the North Cascades National Park. This airline provides daily service along this long lake from the town of Chelan to Stehekin. Flights take visitors past the sheer cliffs surrounding the lake and over thick forested hills. For those meeting other trips, Stehekin Air operates scheduled flights to meet wilderness packers and other tour operators in the vicinity.

For more details, contact: Stehekin Air Service, Box 21, Stehekin, WA 98852; (509) 682-5065.

12

SOARING
WITH EAGLES

Have you ever stood on top of a hill and watched as a child threw a paper airplane into the air? The plane raced silently forward gaining altitude because of the force of the child's throw. Then its nose would tip downward until it gained enough speed, when it would rise again to repeat the process.

Or, have you ever watched a large hawk glide through the air for several minutes never once beating its wings? From the ground, the bird appears to sail on the wind, only tilting its wings to control speed and direction. Soaring birds rise in the air even on the stillest of days and never seem to waste any energy.

There is a sport that parallels these experiences. It combines the graceful flight of the eagle with the dynamics of a perfect paper airplane. In the cockpit of a modern sailplane, you can drift silently through the air, rising on the same drafts and currents that birds have used for millions of years. And, for that matter, it's not uncommon to capture a top view of a hawk, or fly in formation with the birds as they rise in a thermal air current.

This graceful experience of soaring is very much an adventure. Even seasoned pilots are amazed by the versatility of these long-winged craft. And as they fly it is hard to remember that they don't have any man-made method of propulsion. After releasing from the tow plane, gliders remain in flight by juggling three basic forces: currents, ridge air, and gravity.

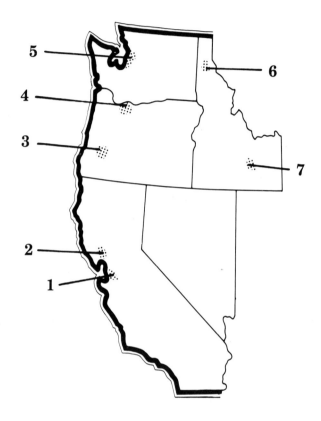

1. *Sky Sailing*
2. *Calistoga Soaring Center*
3. *Emerald Valley Soaring*
4. *Hood River Soaring*
5. *Soaring Unlimited*
6. *Norton Aero*
7. *Queen Bee Air Specialties*

A hawk's-eye view of the Napa Valley from a sailplane being towed to 3000 feet.

Thermals. As the afternoon sun warms the earth, air nearest the surface also heats up and rises. This creates a funnel-like mass of air moving upward in a circular pattern. Some of these thermals can rise several thousand feet before the air stabilizes.

Gliders fly along the fringes of a thermal, turning continually so as to stay near the rising air. Once at the desired altitude, the pilot steers out of the funnel and begins searching for another thermal. To find thermal air, pilots watch the ground terrain. Often these currents are found above large flat rock formations with a southern exposure or open fields. When flying on a straight course, it is very obvious when you encounter a thermal column of rising air. The plane tends to suddenly move upward. In many cases, pilots will bank into a turn and try to climb a little higher.

Ridge Air. Throughout the Northwest offshore winds prevail during spring and summer afternoons. These winds can be powerful and when they encounter a hillside or other steep formation, they rise up over it. Gliders often fly along ridge lines. A talented pilot can achieve very high altitudes for several hours by taking advantage of these currents. Because of the positions of the mountains throughout the West and the uniformity of the prevailing winds, this is one of the main techniques used in cross-country soaring.

On a recent flight, we released from the tow plane at approximately 3,100 feet. Our pilot was a seasoned professional with several hundred hours in the cockpit, and my 5-year-old daughter and I were along for the ride in the back. Glancing over his shoulder, the pilot asked my daughter if she enjoyed roller coaster rides. She answered with a resounding yes. With this, we banked into a sharp turn and headed toward the face of a mountain. As we drew closer, I could see individual hikers on the trail to the top and several people with picnic blankets spread along the grassy knolls. I began wondering how close we were going to get when suddenly we started to climb. Our speed remained just over 60 miles per hour and we were going up. I had to remind myself that this plane had no engines!

Our pilot had given several rides that day before us and encountered strong updrafts from the air rising over this ridge. As I glanced at the altimeter in front of us, I was astonished to see that we had climbed another thousand feet. And then the roller coaster ride really began, which brings us to . . .

Gravity. For all intents and purposes, what goes up usually comes down. But, how could gravity be used to cause a glider to climb?

To understand the effect, consider how the wings work on a plane to cause lift. In very simplified terms, the shape and curve of the top portion of the wing causes a change in air pressure. As air passes above and below the wing, the pressure is less on the top and greater on the bottom, causing lift. Several other factors such as gravity, thrust, and drag affect lift. To create and control this pressure change at will, engines were mounted on airplanes to force the wing through the air.

When the air is somewhat still, gliders accomplish this "propulsion" with the help of Newton's discovery. Recall my first flight. We had just encountered ridge air and climbed nicely to 4,000 feet. The pilot guided us onto a different course and into still air. As our airspeed dropped, he dipped us into a steep dive. The force of gravity caused us to accelerate and, thereby,

The ride in a high-performance glider is as close as most of us will get to experiencing a flight in a jet fighter.

forced the wings through the air. This resulted in the pressure change we just discussed and up we bobbed, much like a cork in water.

A HIGHLY MANEUVERABLE ADVENTURE

As if simply staying in the air were not impressive enough, these sleek-bodied planes can accomplish a variety of aerobatic maneuvers. When I climbed into the cockpit for my very first ride, I was fitted with a full restraint harness and then the canopy was shut. The first impression I had at this point was that I was about to experience what a jet fighter pilot feels.

As we started down the runway on the end of a tow cable, I knew I was not to be disappointed and the glider lifted off before the tow plane. We climbed through relatively stable air, then cresting 3,000 feet the tow plane dipped its wings, rocking gently from side to side as a signal to release the cable. We were on our own, soaring up a thermal beneath a high tower of clouds. As we climbed another 1,500 feet, the pilot tipped the nose and we swooped down much as an eagle would have toward the top of a hill. I was amazed by the control we had as we leveled out over a herd of mountain goats. The dark rings of their horns were clearly visible and I could almost make out the color of their eyes.

From here we caught ridge air and climbed again. Near the edge of the mountain, the pilot tipped the plane into a 60-degree bank. It seemed as though our airspeed dropped to near zero as we appeared to pivot completely around. "See that tall oak?" the pilot called back to me. As we banked into another turn, the downward wing remained pointed at the tree through the entire turn.

We then followed the ridge back and forth until we had reached just under 5,000 feet. Turning away from the mountains, we started our glide back to the airport. Along the way, I experienced the true thrill of a high-performance sailplane. The pilot dipped us into a steep dive and then pulled up while rolling the plane upside-down. The earth had replaced the sky, and I felt disoriented by the sudden change. My 5 year old, who was next to me, was laughing and calling for more. The plane maneuvered sharply toward the ground into a half-loop. "We're taking about three G's now!" the pilot shouted. I was forced back into the seat and my cheeks were tugged back. We completed the wingover upright and flew back toward the mountain. "Ready for another?" the pilot asked. My daughter shouted her approval, and once again the horizon rolled over as we completed a second wingover.

SOARING THE NORTHWEST

Soaring makes for a great afternoon adventure. There are several centers near most of the major cities of the Northwest where sky sailing is practiced. Most of the pilots are private owners who participate in the sport as a hobby. But each of these centers offers rides and flight instruction for those who

Gliding to a perfect one-point touchdown.

want to fly with the hawks. Every ride does not have to be as thrilling as a full acrobatic flight. Most of the centers listed in the following section offer scenic excursions or high-performance flights. It is advisable to call ahead for reservations.

Sky Sailing/California. 44999 Christy Street, Fremont, CA 94538; (415) 656-9900. Located 40 miles south of San Francisco, this company offers standard and high-performance rides, full instruction, and sail plane rentals.

Calistoga Soaring Center/California. 1546 Lincoln Ave., Calistoga, CA 94515; (707) 942-5592. This center is located in the northern tip of the Napa Valley, the prime wine growing area of the state. Open 7 days a week, Calistoga Soaring offers standard scenic flights, the "top gun" flight, full instruction, and rentals. Reservations are strongly recommended during the summer season.

Emerald Valley Soaring/Oregon. Daniels Field, 840 W. 21st Ave., Eugene, OR 97405; (503) 686-0640. This private club offers introductory rides on weekends between May and October. The organization's membership is open to people interested in the sport. Aside from rides, they offer instruction and equipment rentals.

Hood River Soaring/Oregon. Hood River Airport, 3600 Airport Ave., Hood River, OR 97031; (503) 386-1732. The town of Hood River sits in the shadow of the great mountain at the intersection of two major thoroughfares, Interstate 84 and State Route 35. This center is an easy drive from downtown Portland along the scenic Columbia River. Rides are offered year-round on weekends. You can easily make a day-trip to this soaring site. Take the Columbia River Scenic Highway east from Troutdale. There are several parks and dramatic waterfalls along the steep cliffs that make up the walls of the gorge. An early morning stop and short hike at the Multinomah Falls is well worth the time, then after a picnic lunch, it's on to the soaring center for an adventure-filled ride.

Soaring Unlimited/Washington. 12422 68th Ave. N.E., Kirkland, WA 98033; (206) 823-6500. Conveniently located across Lake Washington from Seattle, this center offers a full line of soaring services. Rides are offered daily between March and November.

Norton Aero/Idaho. Henley Aerodome, Rte. 1, Box 98, Athol ID 83801; (208) 683-2581. Located 15 miles north of Coeur d'Alene, this center provides rides over some of the most dramatic scenery in the Continental U.S. Open year round, they also offer private instruction and rentals.

Queen Bee Air Specialties/Idaho. Rigby Airport, P.O. Box 245, Rigby, ID 83442; (208) 745-7654. This center serves the southern portion of the state near the community of Idaho Falls. Their services include rides, instruction, and rentals.

13

HOT AIR ADVENTURES IN THE CLOUDS

From the days of our childhood, countless adventures seemed to begin or end in the gondola of a mammoth hot air balloon. And today, the daring experience of the first aviators is maintained in glorious tradition throughout the Northwest. Every detail is remembered. On a recent flight, just as the balloon was heading for a landing on a grassy hill, the wind currents shifted and we put down behind a modest ranch home. The pilot was careful to guide the balloon beyond the garden and touched down near the crest of a small hill. He gave the burners one last shot, and the flame heated the air while the deafening roar blotted out any other sounds. As the silence returned, a dog barked at us from the side of the house. It was a large German Shepherd, tethered to a chain.

"Just like in days of old," the pilot remarked as the ground crew exchanged fuel bottles for fresh ones. "In the early days," the pilot continued, "the aviators of France would fly their balloons for a short distance over the vineyards. They would inevitably land in some farmer's field. Only, back then, the farmers were very suspicious and believed the mammoth balloons were demons. They would often unleash their dogs and attack the aviators with farm tools. It was then that the tradition of exchanging wine and song was born."

"The winds have welcomed you with softness; the sun has blessed you with warm hands; you have flown so high and so

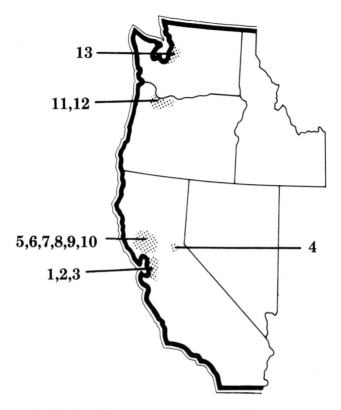

1. *Farnham Enterprises*
2. *Hot Air Unlimited*
3. *Balloon Excelsior*
4. *Big Sky Balloons*
5. *Napa Valley Balloons*
6. *Once in a Lifetime*
7. *Napa's Great Balloon Escape*
8. *Adventures Aloft*
9. *Hot Air and Company*
10. *Skyline Balloons*
11. *Oregon Balloon Adventures*
12. *Atmospheric Adventures*
13. *The Seattle Balloon Depot*

well that God has joined you in laughter and has set you gently back again in the loving arms of Mother Earth." And so was the aviator's poem recited by the crew as the pilot once again ignited the burners to rise up and become a part of the wind.

A hot air balloon rises
on the morning air . . .

. . . to capture a breathtaking view of the valley below.

A balloon being inflated and readied for take-off.

On the ground, a note was left at the door of the house to greet the absent owners upon their return. It thanked them for the brief but unscheduled use of their property, and prayed they enjoy the bottle of California champagne affixed to the parchment.

History repeats itself. From that fateful Parisian morning in 1783 when the brothers Montgolfier along with the King of France and a crowd of over 400,000 watched the Marquis d'Arlandes fly for the first time in one of their balloons, a tradition was born. Man would conquer the skies. In the years following, hot air balloons—called Montgolfiers—were built in a variety of sizes and shapes. Some possessed large wicker baskets and one, named *Le Giant,* held an enclosed wicker house for passengers. Simultaneous to these developments, another Frenchman built and launched the first gas-filled balloon. Using hydrogen to fill the envelope, this balloon was able to stay aloft much longer and lacked the stench of smoke from the fire used to heat the air.

There remained one major obstacle to the French aeronauts' conquest of lighter-than-air flight: a workable steering system.

They were accomplished at getting the balloons into the air but, once up, they had no control over where they would land. They tried fans, oars, and other devices with no luck until the advent of the gasoline engine. With a propeller driven by a light-weight motor and a rudder to control the draft, they were finally able to steer the balloons. The combination of steering and the use of hydrogen gas led to the development of the first dirigibles. But, gradually, fixed-wing aircraft replaced the services that dirigibles and balloons once provided. The age of aeronauts appeared to be over.

Developments over the last decade in nylon fabric and the use of liquid propane burners to heat the air have given a rebirth to this age-old sport. The remainder of this chapter examines the new-world aeronauts and locations throughout the Northwest for aeronautical adventures.

LIGHTER THAN AIR

An adventure in the clouds begins at the crack of dawn, when the first rays of light reach the valley, the birds awaken and begin foraging for breakfast, and a family of squirrels emerge from their burrow to collect nuts. The wind is still and the morning silent.

This is the best time for balloon flights. Before the sun has its chance to heat the ground, creating thermal updrafts, the aviator can be assured that the air will be moving in gentle layers. If the wind is too strong, control of the balloon becomes that much more challenging. Since a ground crew will chase the balloon and assist with landing, it is important to leave as little as possible to chance.

A suitable clearing is selected, and the ground crew uses a lift to lower the gondola from the back of the truck. The wicker and leather basket is built around a triangular base. Its high walls conceal the controls and six fuel cartridges. The framework supports two large burners. Laying the basket on its side, the ground crew begins clipping on the nylon leads that will attach to the envelope (balloon). At this point, one person usually hoists a duffel bag from the back of the truck. It looks as if it might contain a large tent; certainly not a hot air bal-

Thumbs up! The pilot lights the burners to heat the air in the envelope.

loon that stands 73 feet tall and over 50 feet wide when filled. But this is in fact the balloon.

The future passengers watch in utter amazement as the envelope is stretched from the bag to its full length on the ground and carefully unfolded. No colors appear at this point, and a few of the guests express their dismay at the drab appearance of the balloon. "The brochure didn't look anything like this," one woman comments. A crew member winks at her and gives a knowing grin.

Once the rigging has been connected to the gondola, a large fan is positioned at the mouth of the balloon. One guest supports the machine, while two others hold open the skirt around the base of the envelope. The gas engine on the fan starts with a roar and almost instantly the envelope comes alive and begins growing. Its colors burst to life as the air is forced inside. While the passengers and crew tend to the inflating giant, the pilot takes this moment to crawl into the basket and begin his pre-flight checks.

At the point when the balloon is fully inflated, resting on its side, the pilot orders the fan secured. The crew moves the fan clear and then takes up a position beyond the crown of the balloon. As though expecting a tug-o-war, they line up and grab hold of the rope coming from the top of the envelope. The ground crew chief gives the thumbs up and the pilot lights the burners. He hits the blast valve on one and a jet of fire shoots toward the open envelope. After only a few seconds, the balloon starts to right itself against gravity. The crew holds fast to the rope, fighting a losing tug-o-war with the mammoth force—but their goal is only to slow the ascent of the balloon until it is upright. This requires a great amount of heel dragging until the gondola is upright. On the sidelines, the guests watch in utter amazement that something this massive could have come from such a small duffel bag.

Once upright, the balloon's colors radiate their full glory in the morning sun. The adventure begins as a maximum of six guests join the pilot in the gondola. The remaining guests travel with the flight crew and chase after the balloon on the ground. They will get their turn in an hour, after the first flight puts down and the passengers change places.

The pilot instructs his travelers on a few simple safety precautions and apologizes that he may have to cut conversations off by hitting the blast valves. As soon as the guests are ready, he opens one of the valves for a few seconds and the balloon lifts off. To the passengers, the sensation of flight begins only a few inches above the ground. The craft moves off as the pilot ignites the burners once again to increase altitude.

Climbing gradually, the pilot quickly demonstrates how he can select a course by choosing a moving layer of air. One passenger notices how warm it is getting inside the gondola and asks why he cannot feel the wind. The pilot grins and says, "We *are* the wind." This becomes increasingly evident as the dark shadow of the balloon skirts across the ground below, but none of the passengers feels anything except the warmth from the burners when they're fired.

On a recent flight, our pilot demonstrated his control over the craft. He lowered us until we were only a few feet above the ground in a farmer's orchard. The fruit dangling from the limbs of the black walnut trees was so close we could tell

which were ripe enough for harvesting. The pilot then demonstrated true "nape of the earth" flying. He maintained an altitude of two feet. As we encountered a tree or fence, he would jerk the blast valve open so as to pass over the obstacle, then let the envelope cool and drop us back to the two-foot level. After hopping several trees and a four-foot-high fence, we were convinced. The adventure continued as we rose 2,000 feet for a bird's eye view of the valley.

NORTHWESTERN BALLOON ADVENTURES

There are locations throughout the region where visitors can spend an hour or so aloft, drifting with the wind. In searching for the perfect aeronautical adventure, you will find that balloons and wine go hand in hand. This is no doubt due to their colorful relationship throughout history. You can safely bet that there will be a balloon company in close proximity to most wine producing areas.

I have selected representative companies within the region as a "shopping list." Be assured that there are many more companies operating than there is space to list them. Therefore, as with several of the other adventures in this guide, you should view this list as a starting point.

When you speak to the representative of the companies, be sure to ask a few questions. First, ask how large they are. The biggest in the area is not always the best. I have found that trips where the owner is also the pilot offer the best in service. If the firm is large, their pilots may be contract fliers. This is not really something to avoid, but you may want to consider asking a few additional questions about the pilot's personality, training, and past employers if this is the case.

Find out how long the company has been in business and how many flights per month they make. Ask for a few local references in your area that you can call. Also inquire as to what else is included with the trip. Many serve a champagne brunch and have a small ceremony to commemorate your flight.

The burners blast with a loud rumble, and the balloon rises effortlessly into the air.

Lastly, try to find out how many flights they plan on the day of your trip. Since it is difficult to photograph the adventure from inside the basket, it makes the trip just that much more exciting if you can ride with the ground crew for a while. This is when you'll get the best photo opportunities. One factor in favor of the larger companies is that they often fly more than one balloon on a busy weekend.

The following is a list of various balloon companies operating in the Northwest. You may wonder why the list seems heavily weighted toward California. According to a recent survey, over 10% of all privately held hot air balloons are in the Golden State. This may be a result of the recent growth in ballooning over the major wine growing regions of the state.

Farnham Enterprises/California. P.O. Box 1617, Morgan Hill, CA 95037; (408) 778-1945. This company offers a variety of adventure and charter flights in the Santa Clara Valley south of San Francisco. They specialize in champagne flights, moonlight flights, and over-the-mountain flights.

Hot Air Unlimited/California. 137 Hamilton Ave., Suite 208, Campbell, CA 95088; (408) 379-2122. This company offers early morning balloon flights over the wine growing region of the southern Santa Clara Valley.

Balloon Excelsior/California. 1241 High Street, Oakland, CA 94601; (415) 261-4222. This company offers morning flights through the Livermore and San Joaquin Valleys in central California. Special packages include a custom-designed gourmet weekend during which a group can charter the balloon for a weekend adventure, including meals. Choosing items from their "Command Cuisine" menu is a gastronomic adventure in itself.

Big Sky Balloons/California. P.O. Box 5665, Auburn, CA 95694; (916) 961-0220. This is one of the few outfitters offering flights over the California Gold Country. Their champagne flights take off from different locations in the Sierra Foothills and take in the vast beauty of the Sierras. They also offer a variety of combination tours along with Lincoln House Bed and Breakfast Inn and American River Recreation, a whitewater rafting outfitter. For one reasonable price, guests can enjoy the relaxed luxury of the inn, with an early morning balloon flight and a wild rafting adventure in the afternoon on the American River.

Napa Valley Balloons/California. P.O. Box 2860, Yountville, CA 94599; (707) 253-2224. With some of the most beautiful vineyards in the West as a backdrop, this company enjoys a fine reputation for bringing their guests an excellent fantasy adventure. They operate a fleet of six balloons, and on busy weekends, you might be lucky enough to watch them all take off. Their flights begin early in the morning and last for approximately an hour, concluding with a champagne celebration and gourmet picnic lunch.

Once In A Lifetime/California. P.O. Box 795, Calistoga, CA 94515; (707) 942-6541. This company flies over the Northern Napa Valley town of Calistoga, famous for its mineral water. The company's owners take pride in also being the pilots on every trip and bringing something special to the adventure of lighter than air flight. Their trips conclude at the Mountain View Hotel in downtown Calistoga, where the chef prepares a gourmet brunch from Once In A Lifetime's private menu.

Napa's Great Balloon Escape/California. P.O. Box 4197, Napa, CA 94558; (707) 253-0860. This company offers a personalized great escape complete with continental pre-flight breakfast and a champagne photo party afterwards.

Adventures Aloft/California. P.O. Box 2500, Yountville, CA 94599; (707) 255-8688. This company flies seven days a week from Yountville in the heart of the California wine growing region. This is one of the larger companies in the Napa Valley. They also provide balloon sales, flight training, and promotional displays for those who are interested.

Hot Air and Company/California. 10998 Peaks Pike Road, Sebastopol, CA 95427; (707) 823-6892. This company operates champagne balloon flights year round in California's other wine growing area, the Sonoma Valley.

Skyline Balloons/California. P.O. Box 2152, Santa Rosa, CA 95405; (707) 544-6110. This company hosts flights aboard a balloon with the design of the San Francisco skyline on its side. They fly seven days a week. Terrie Gershman and her husband pilot the balloon and operate the company with the intent of bringing a special, personalized flavor to every trip.

Oregon Balloon Adventures/Oregon. 2221 S.W. First Street, Suite 823, Portland, OR 97201; (503) 648-6769. Jeff Shields and Susan James operate two balloons in Northern Oregon. Together, they try to provide unique experiences for their guests. For those inclined to experience a new thrill, try their flight over Portland. This deluxe trip offers a new and exciting aereal view of one of the most attractive Northwestern cities.

`*Atmospheric Adventures/Oregon.* P.O. Box 1054, Hillsboro, OR 97124; (503) 648-6769. Located a few miles west of Portland, this company offers travelers flights through the northern Willamette Valley. As with several of the companies, this is a small privately held outfitter that prides itself on giving something extra to their clients.

The Seattle Balloon Depot/Washington. 16138 N.E. 87th Ave., Redmond, WA 98065; (206) 881-9699. This company beckons guests to come and indulge in a fantasy flight. Offering trips over some of the most beautiful terrain in all of Washington, the Balloon Depot's clients will not be disappointed. Complete champagne flights and group rates are available.

14

ADVENTURE— A PRESCRIPTION FOR STRESS

This book has presented several adventure alternatives, and each has similar therapeutic qualities. They all occur outdoors, involve physical activity, provide an opportunity to meet new friends, and lastly, they challenge us to succeed. At the conclusion of these trips, we all feel a degree of escape from the cares of our workaday world.

This effect was never more evident than during a recent cycling trip through the California wine country. Traveling with a group of 26 other people, it was a golden opportunity to meet new friends. The outfitter on this guided expedition hosted a dinner the night before our ride was to begin. Traveling alone, I had a unique opportunity to listen to the conversations around me and make a few mental notes about the people.

Most of my fellow riders at the dinner spoke to their respective partners and the people around them about their own jobs or personal pastimes. They focused on the stressful, negative aspects of their lives. And the evening proceeded.

Bright and early the next morning, we joined again in the same dining room for breakfast and a briefing on the day's route. From the looks in the people's eyes and their expressions, it was already evident that the night's sleep had begun a relaxing trend. Instead of stifling conversation about problems, the talk now was about gear and equipment and the adventure to come.

The ride that day was over rolling terrain and included several stops at wineries and scenic overlooks. At the halfway point, we were to picnic at the top of a quarter-mile-long grade that would have had a mountain goat huffing and puffing. After being used to generally level terrain for over 16 miles, this sudden 6% grade seemed insurmountable. As riders encountered the hill, there were cheers of support. Some had to dismount and walk for a distance but the others rallied to urge them on. As you might imagine, by lunch this group of riders had begun to form a friendship that would carry them through the weekend. The Oakville Grade was only the first obstacle to be overcome, for on the very next morning at the three-and-a-half-mile mark, there was another hill to be conquered. And on this occasion, the group attacked it as a team. It no longer mattered whether you were a doctor, oil company executive, waiter, business manager, or janitor . . . you all worked toward a common objective. The stronger riders rode at a slower pace and urged on the weaker members; at the top, those who finished waited for the others and cheered them on. Then everyone enjoyed the downhill portion as a team. By the end of the weekend, each individual was better for the effort. Not so much from the physical aspect of exercise, but from the mental recess granted by the exertion.

As more and more of us have learned, exercise helps prevent heart attacks, aids weight control, instills a feeling of well being, and enhances creativity. In their text, *The Sports Medicine Book,* the authors show how physical activity helps improve mood. This has sometimes been described by athletes as a "high" from exercise. According to Mirkin and Hoffman, the authors, this is caused by physiologic reactions, one of which is the release of norepinephrine into the blood stream. This hormone is necessary for the transmission of messages along certain nerves of the brain. Typically, people who are happy have high levels of norepinephrine.

Well, you don't have to become a marathon runner to enjoy the therapeutic effects of physical exercise. Though there is no substitute for a healthy and fit body, you can combine a few activities into a weekend and enjoy a retreat away from your worries and work. I believe a key ingredient is to escape to an environment that insulates us from the stressful "real" world.

After searching the Northwest for adventures of all kinds, I set about planning a few itineraries specifically as antidotes for stress. As you will note, each of the trips described in this chapter is near a major city in the region. Each sample trip has been categorized by season and the city nearby.

THE AUTHOR'S CHOICE

Boise, Idaho

Winter. This portion of the country is a winter wonderland. For a weekend get-away, I would elect to stay and ski at Busterback Ranch. The accommodations are limited to 20 guests, just enough to enjoy the perfect holiday escaping from it all. See chapter on cross-country skiing for details.

Summer. Idaho is no disappointment in the summer season. This state boasts one of the largest wilderness preserves in the continental United States.

Shepp Ranch, Idaho offers the perfect environment to forget your worries and get back to basics. The ranch is situated at the base of America's second deepest gorge where Crooked Creek meets the Salmon River. It is surrounded by 256,000 acres of wilderness. There are no roads, no noise, no radios, no telephones, and no motorized vehicles. Guests are either shuttled in from the Boise airport by private plane, or experience a jet boat ride up the Salmon River. Only 24 guests can visit the ranch at any one time. This is a recreational paradise. The ranch hands make arrangements for their guests to enjoy hiking, horseback riding, rafting, jet boating, trout fishing, and swimming.

When you arrive here, take off your watch and sit a spell on the porch of your cabin. Let the world pass you by for a while instead of trying to keep pace. For more details, contact: *Shepp Ranch*, P.O. Box 5466, Boise, ID 83705.

Aside from ranching, Idaho is a whitewater wonderland. There are several rafting outfitters throughout the state who offer trips on some of the finest rapids in the United States. Canyons Incorporated offers 5- and 6-day trips down the Salmon River. These trips include air transportation from Mc-

Call, Idaho to the town of Salmon, and then a wild trip down the river. Most of these trips involve camping along the banks of the River of No Return, but they do run special 4-day lodging trips, on which their guests enjoy the finest wilderness lodges each evening. For more details, contact the owner of *Canyons Incorporated,* Susan Bechdel, P.O. Box 823, McCall, ID 83638; (208) 634-4303.

Seattle, Washington

Winter. The ultimate adventure is to ski the back lands of the Olympic National Park. Tudor Inn in Port Angeles, Washington provides the perfect weekend package for people in metropolitan Seattle.

You begin your adventure with a ferry ride across Puget Sound to Bremerton. From here you make the hour-and-a-half drive up to Port Angeles and check in with Jerry and Jan Glass. At the same time, find out whether the Sol Duc resort and spa is open. The Glasses can make any arrangements for your visit to this unique volcanic attraction in the Olympic National Park. This makes an excellent side-trip after skiing, if the roads are clear. Then plan on relaxed evenings at the Tudor Inn. For more details on this trip, refer to the chapter on skiing adventures; or contact the Glasses directly at *Tudor Inn,* 1108 S. Oak Ave., Port Angeles, WA 98362; (206) 452-3138.

Summer. Put yourself in the trusting hands of Backroads Bicycle Touring for an adventure around Puget Sound. This tour offers the very best of the jewel of the Northwest. Meeting in Ancortes, the first day's tour takes riders into the heart of the San Juan Islands. From here, you travel over rolling hills and enjoy beautiful vistas of the Sound. While riding along an optional loop, you might be lucky enough to catch a glimpse of a killer whale swimming offshore.

Backroads takes care of all your cycling needs on one of their tours. While on the road, their van and supply trailer patrol the route to help any riders who may experience mechanical difficulties. Also, at least one guide functions as a sweep-rider at the back of the group to provide any additional support. All meals are provided and prepared by the guides or served in the finest restaurants along the course. Lodging is provided at local inns that offer a flavor of the local atmosphere. Not enough can be said about Backroads' guides. They work from the break of dawn until well after sunset to give their guests the best vacation experience.

For more details about the Puget Sound adventure, contact: *Backroads Bicycle Touring,* P.O. Box 1626, San Leandro, CA 94577; (415) 895-1783.

Portland/Eugene/Springfield, Oregon

Winter. One of the finest recreational adventures is found just a few miles north of the Washington border. At the foot of Mount Adams, a few miles southeast of Mount St. Helens, an Oregon outfitter has discovered a winter adventure that combines the excitement of the back country and an age-old mode of transportation. Wilderness Freighters operates weekend dogsled adventures to cabins located along the base of Mount Adams. John and Lynn Simonson welcome guests along with their teams of Alaskan malamute dogs. Starting from the Flying-L Ranch, guests load their gear in a snow cat and start off into the wilderness. Every few miles, guests rotate out of the snow cat and into the dogsled. By lunch, you arrive at the first cabin and a piping hot meal is ready and waiting. Once you've warmed up, one of the several ski guides leads small groups on cross country ski tours in the surrounding area.

For more details on this trip, refer to the skiing chapter, or contact John Simonson, *Wilderness Freighters,* 2166 SE 142nd Ave., Portland, OR; (503) 761-7428.

Summer. At the base of the Willamette Valley, a few miles south of Eugene, Oregon, the Rogue River crashes westward on its course to the Pacific Ocean. This is prime whitewater country for those who like the waves big and exciting and the civilized environment of a country lodge at night. O.A.R.S./ Sobek International Expeditions offers just such a get-away package. Their "Rogue Lodge" trip combines the excitement of a whitewater expedition with fashionable accommodations.

The Rogue Lodge trip is offered in the spring and once in the fall. Trips later in the summer are possible by special arrangement. For further information, contact: *O.A.R.S./Sobek Expe-*

ditions, P.O. Box 87, Angels Camp, CA 95222; (209) 736-4677 or (800) 2344-3284 from outside California.

San Francisco/Sacramento, California

Winter. One of the ultimate winter weekend retreats is at Yosemite National Park. Only three and a half hours from San Francisco by car, the Yosemite Valley in winter can only be described as magnificent. As you enter, the Valley walls rise several thousand feet above you, and each of the majestic peaks is sprinkled with a light frosting of snow. The more gradual slopes are covered with their winter coats. This contrast of dark granite highlighted by the snow and blue sky provides many photographic opportunities.

Several attractive full-service lodges remain open during the winter months along the Valley. Each provides cozy rooms and offers a hearty cuisine for guests. And in the mornings, shuttles leave on a regular schedule to Badger Pass, the alpine and cross-country ski areas. From this point, cross-country skiers can travel to many of the major geologic attractions in the Park with a guide or on their own following a marked trail. Maps and more information can be obtained from the *Yosemite Park and Curry Company,* Yosemite National Park, CA 95389; (209) 372-1000.

Summer. A favorite summer trip also takes place near the Sierra Nevada mountains about 200 miles east of San Francisco along Interstate 80 at the old gold mining town of Auburn. Here, Big Sky Balloons has combined the best of sea and air adventures into a fantasy, get-away weekend. This unique package includes one night's lodging at the Lincoln House bed-and-breakfast inn near downtown Auburn, a hot air balloon trip the next morning, followed by a whitewater expedition on the American River that afternoon.

After completing this adventure weekend, I like to conclude my visit with an additional night's lodging or a drive further into the Mother Lode. The town of Murpheys is located a few miles east of Angels Camp along State Highway 4. The Murpheys' Hotel is located along the main thoroughfare. Visitors can have their choice of antique rooms in the original structure from the mid-1800's or modern, motor-inn accommodations across the courtyard. And, if the prior morning's adventures were not enough, Mercer Caverns is located a few blocks from the center of town. See the chapter on cave exploration for details on the cavern.

For more information on the adventure package, contact: *Big Sky Balloons,* P.O. Box 5665, Auburn, CA 95604; (916) 961-0220.

For information and reservations for the Murpheys' Hotel, contact the hotel at (209) 728-3444.

There is one more adventure site that, due to its unique setting and provisions for exciting escapes, demands mention. The town of Calistoga, 60 miles north of San Francisco, is the starting point for several adventure trips. Situated in the northern tip of the Napa Valley, Calistoga is in the center of the California wine region and has several natural hot springs.

Soon after the turn of the century, people throughout the West traveled to this remote town to experience the European-style spas. This was a fashionable trend of the time, and several towns similar to Calistoga were scattered throughout the volcanic regions of the West. Once the Second World War engulfed the country, this trend faded along with most of the towns, except Calistoga. Right up to the present, the spas have been maintained in their European elegance.

Calistoga is also a center for several adventure trips: Backroads Bicycle Touring operates weekend cycling adventures from the Mountain View Hotel; Calistoga Soaring Center offers daily glider flights; numerous hot air balloon companies drift over the Napa Valley on champagne flights; and the trailhead up Mount Saint Helena is only a few miles further down the road. Each of these trips is described in the various chapters of this book.

To cap off the perfect Calistoga weekend, consider staying at a couple of the bed-and-breakfast inns. There are several excellent ones to pick from in the nearby area. Two inns stand out near the top of my list in quality and service to adventurers. Their innkeepers know a great deal about local attractions and are more than willing to make reservations for their guests. If you want to go ballooning, take a mud and mineral bath, or take in a few "special" winery tours, just leave the arrangements to them.

Bartels Ranch. Jami Bartels, 1200 Conn Valley Road, Saint Helena, CA 94574; (707) 963-4001. Jami has been living in the Napa Valley for years and her ranch is a romantic retreat.

Foothill House. Michael and Susan Clow, 3037 Foothill Blvd., Calistoga, CA 94515; (707) 942-4102. Michael and Susan welcome their guests to this cozy inn along the north side of town. Under the watchful presence of Mount Saint Helena, this inn is perfectly situated for the weekend adventurer.

After a day cycling or hiking up the flanks of the mountain, there is nothing more relaxing than taking the "full treatment" at one of the many Calistoga spas. I would recommend *Dr. Wilkinson's Hot Springs* located at 1507 Lincoln Ave., next door to the Mountain View Hotel. They offer complete routines, including: mud bath, mineral whirlpool, steam, Indian blanket wrap, and either half-hour or full-hour massage. This is one of the more popular spas, so appointments are strongly recommended. Contact Dr. Wilkinson's at (707) 942-4102.

APPENDIX:

CHAMBERS OF COMMERCE AND TOURISM INFORMATION CENTERS

This appendix lists representative tourist information centers and chambers of commerce in the Northwest. These offices provide callers with the most current information on adventure outfitters, hotel operators, and restaurants. It is important to note that most of these organizations rely on business memberships within their respective communities; therefore, any response will naturally be from one of their members. It is strongly recommended that you call and interview any of the outfitters and guide services. Your safety should not be left to a decision based solely on the fact that a business has joined a chamber of commerce.

INFORMATION SERVICES

California

Statewide Information:
State of California, Department of Commerce, Office of Tourism, 1121 L Street, Suite 103, Sacramento, CA 95814; (916) 322-2881.

Monterey County and Coastal Area:
Monterey Peninsula Chamber of Commerce, 380 Alvarado Street, Monterey, CA 93940; (408) 649-1770.

San Francisco and Bay Area:
San Francisco Convention and Visitors Bureau, P.O. Box 6977, San Francisco, CA 94101; (415) 974-6900.

Delta and San Joaquin Valley Area:
Stockton-San Joaquin Convention and Visitors Bureau, 46 West Fremont Street, Stockton, CA 95202; (209) 943-1987.
Sacramento Convention and Visitors Bureau, 11311 I Street, Sacramento, CA 95814; (916) 442-5542.

Lake Tahoe:
Tahoe North Visitors and Convention Bureau, 850 North Lake Blvd., Tahoe City, CA 95730; (800) 822-5959 or out of state calls: (800) 824-8557.

Yosemite Area:
Yosemite National Park, Yosemite Park National Park, CA 95389; (209) 373-4171.

Mother Lode and Gold Country Area:
El Dorado County Chamber of Commerce, 542 Main Street, Placerville, CA 95667; (916) 626-2344.
Placer County Visitor Information Center, 661 Newcastle Road, Newcastle, CA 95658; (916) 663-2061.

North Coast and Wine Country:
Redwood Empire Association, One Market Plaza, Spear Street

Tower, Suite #1001, San Francisco, CA 94105; (415) 543-8338.

Calistoga Chamber of Commerce, 1458 Lincoln Ave., Calistoga, CA 94515; (707) 942-6333.

Napa Chamber of Commerce, 1900 Jefferson Street, Napa, CA 94559; (707) 226-7455.

North/Central California and Mount Shasta Area:
Shasta-Cascade Wonderland Association, 1250 Parkview Ave., Redding, CA 96001; (916) 243-2643.

Oregon

Statewide Information:
Oregon Economic Development Department, 595 Cottage St., N.E., Salem, OR 97310; (503) 378-3451.

Southern Oregon and Crater Lake Area:
Ashland Visitors and Convention Bureau, P.O. Box 606, Ashland, OR 97520; (503) 482-3486.

Central Oregon:
Bend Visitor and Convention Bureau, 164 N.W. Hawthorne, Bend, OR 97701; 382-3221.

Willamette Valley Area:
Eugene-Springfield Convention and Visitors Bureau, 305 W. 7th Street, Eugene, OR 97401; (800) 452-3670 or outside Oregon: (800) 547-5445.

Springfield Area Chamber of Commerce, P.O. Box 155, Springfield, OR 97477; (503) 746-1651.

Salem Convention and Visitors Association, 1313 Mill St. S.E., Salem, OR 97301; (503) 581-4325.

Eastern Oregon and Hell's Canyon Area:
Ontario Chamber of Commerce, 173 S.W. First Street, Ontario, OR 97914; (503) 889-8012.

Northern Oregon and Columbia River Area:
Greater Portland Convention and Visitors Association, 20 S.W. Salom Ave., Portland, OR 97204; (503) 222-2223.

North Coast Area:
Seaside Chamber of Commerce, P.O. Box 7, Seaside, OR 97138; (503) 738-6391 or inside Oregon: (800) 452-6740.

Washington

Southeastern Area:
Walla Walla Area Chamber of Commerce, Box 644, Walla Walla, WA 99362; (509) 525-0850.

Northeastern Area:
Spokane Regional Convention and Visitors Bureau, W. 301 Main Street, Spokane, WA 99201; (509) 525-0850.

South Central Area:
Yakima Valley Visitors and Convention Bureau, 10 N. 8th Street, Yakima, WA 98902; (509) 575-1300.

North Central and Lake Chelan Area:
Omak Chamber of Commerce, P.O. Box 2087, Omak, WA 98841; (509) 826-1880.

Northern and San Juan Islands:
Anacortes Chamber of Commerce, 1319 Commercial Avenue, Anacortes, WA 98221; (206) 293-3832.

Seattle Area:
Seattle/King County Convention and Visitors Bureau, 666 Stewart Street, Seattle, WA 98101; (206) 447-4240.

Tacoma, Olympia and South Puget Sound Area:
Thurston County Parks and Recreation Department, 529 W. 4th Ave., Olympia, WA 98501; (206) 786-5595.

Southwestern and Mount St. Helens Area:
Tourist Regional Information Program of Southwest Washington, P.O. Box 128, Longview, WA 98632; (206) 577-3321.

Olympic Peninsula and Olympic National Park:
Olympic Peninsula Tourism Council, P.O. Box 303, Port Angeles, WA 98362; (206) 479-3594.

Idaho

Statewide Information:
Idaho Travel Council, Statehouse, Boise, ID 83720; (208) 334-2470 or outside Idaho: (800) 635-7820.

Northern Panhandle, Lake Coeur d'Alene Area:
Coeur d'Alene Chamber of Commerce, P.O. Box 850, Coeur d'Alene, ID 83814; (208) 664-3194.

Lower Panhandle, Lewis and Clark Area:
Riggins Chamber of Commerce, P.O. Box 289, Riggins, ID 83549; (208) 328-3613.

Boise and Salmon River Area:
Boise Convention and Visitors Bureau, P.O. Box 2106, Boise, ID 83701; (208) 344-7777 or (800) 635-5240.

South Central and Sun Valley Area:
Sun Valley-Ketchum Chamber of Commerce, P.O. Box 2420, Ketchum, ID 83353; (208) 726-4471.
Twin Falls Chamber of Commerce, 323 Shoshone Street N., Twin Falls, ID 83301; (208) 733-3974.

Southeastern and Minnetonka Cave Area:
Lava Hot Springs Chamber of Commerce, P.O. Box 668, Lava Hot Springs, ID 83246; (208) 776-5221.

Sawtooth Recreation Area:
Stanley-Sawtooth Chamber of Commerce, P.O. Box 45, Stanley, ID 83278.
Rigby Chamber of Commerce, P.O. Box 327, Rigby ID 83442; (208) 745-6677.

GEOGRAPHICAL INDEX

San Francisco, CA	Sky Ridge Ranch	133
San Francisco, CA	Balloon Excelsior	192
San Francisco, CA	Farnham Enterprises	192
San Francisco, CA	Hot Air Unlimited	192
San Francisco, CA	Portola Valley Loop	35
San Francisco, CA	Golden Gate Bridge/Sausalito	38
Seattle, WA	Mazama Country Inn	121
Seattle, WA	Mt. Ranier	121
Seattle, WA	High Country Packers	134
Seattle, WA	North Cascades River	151
Seattle, WA	Downstream River Runners	151
Seattle, WA	Lake Union Air	173
Seattle, WA	Soaring Unlimited	182
Seattle, WA	Seattle Balloon Depot	194
Seattle, WA	Gardner Cave	20
Seattle, WA	Burke Gilman Bike Trail	54
Sequoia Natl Park	Cedar Grove Pack Station	133
Shasta	Castle Lake Nordic Center	117
Shasta	Marble Mt. Wilderness Packers	133
Shasta	Shasta Llamas	134
Shasta	Turtle River Rafting	150
Shasta	Shasta Caverns	16
Shasta	Lassen/Burney Falls	47
Shasta	Mt. Lassen	75
Shasta	Castle Crags	77
Southern Oregon	Oregon Caves Nat'l Monument	14
Southern Oregon	Lava River Caves	16
Southern Washington	Trail Blazer Llamas	134
Yosemite	Badger Pass/Yosemite	114
Yosemite	Lost Valley Pack Station	133
Yosemite	Half Dome/Yosemite	69